JESUS

# JESUS

## a Life
## in Pictures

*His
Complete
Story
Interwoven
from the
Biblical
Gospels*

GEORGE W.
KNIGHT

BARBOUR
PUBLISHING

ISBN 978-1-63609-239-3

Cover images: Wikimedia

Published by Barbour Publishing, Inc., 1810 Barbour Drive, Uhrichsville, Ohio 44683, www.barbourbooks.com

*Our mission is to inspire the world with the life-changing message of the Bible.*

Printed in China.

# CONTENTS

# CHAPTER 4

## Jesus' Early Ministry in the Region of Galilee . . . . . . . . . . . . . . . . . . . . 55

# CHAPTER 5

## The Sermon on the Mount . . . . . . . . . . . . . . . . . . . . . . . . . . . . . . . . 71

## CHAPTER 6

# CHAPTER 7

# CHAPTER 8

## CHAPTER 9

Jesus' Ministry in the Region Beyond the Jordan River ........... 155

## CHAPTER 10

Events from the Triumphal Entry to the Garden of Gethsemane ... 181

## CHAPTER 11

Jesus' Arrest, Trial, and Crucifixion . . . . . . . . . . . . . . . . . . . . . . . 217

## CHAPTER 12

### Jesus' Resurrection and Ascension ....................237

# JESUS,
## a Life in Pictures

What do you get when you interweave the accounts of Jesus' life from all four Gospels into one seamless narrative? You get a more complete story of His life than is possible from reading each Gospel in isolation.

And then what happens when you enrich this story with classical pictures from Christian history and other sources? You get a book that yields a dramatic portrait of Jesus in images and words—*Jesus, a Life in Pictures*—a treasury of information and inspiration.

To make a good thing even better, the book's printed text preserves the best of the old while adding something new. The words come from an adaptation of the King James Bible known as the Simplified KJV. This refinement of the beloved translation has produced a text that is easier to understand. But it preserves the beauty and familiarity of the original King James.

The book divides Jesus' life story into twelve chapters. These cover the events that occurred from the time before He was born to the days of His crucifixion, resurrection, and ascension. These chapters in turn are organized into 250 individual sections of scripture. These detailed sections should sharpen your focus on the various parts of His public ministry.

The four Gospels—Matthew, Mark, Luke, and John—often contain accounts of the same events in Jesus' life. When this is the case, only the most complete or informative narrative is printed in the book. Differences among the Gospel accounts are pointed out in an accompanying sidebar, or parallel passages are cited so you can compare the similarities and differences yourself.

A list of the miracles and parables of Jesus appears at the back of the book. Follow the cross-references to find the place in the book where these accounts appear. This feature will allow you to do a quick study of these important events in His life.

Another handy feature is the maps section, also at the back of the book. These maps will direct you to most of the places where Jesus healed and taught during His ministry in Galilee, Judea, Jerusalem, and beyond.

This book goes out with the prayer that it will bring you closer to Him of whom it was said, "He has done all things well. He makes both the deaf to hear and the mute to speak" (Mark 7:37).

GEORGE W. KNIGHT
*Hartselle, Alabama*

# CHAPTER 1

## Preparation for the Birth of Jesus

*Long before He came to earth, Jesus existed as God's co-creator of the universe. His coming was also foretold by the prophets of the Old Testament. And—closer to the event itself—a peasant girl named Mary was selected as the agent through which He made His entrance into the world.*

# 1. JESUS' ETERNAL EXISTENCE

In the beginning was the Word, and the Word was with God, and the Word was God. The same was in the beginning with God. All things were made by Him, and without Him nothing was made that was made. In Him was life, and the life was the light of men. And the light shines in darkness, and the darkness did not comprehend it.

There was a man sent from God whose name was John. The same came as a witness, to bear witness of the Light, that through him all men might believe. He was not that Light but was sent to bear witness of that Light. That was the true Light that gives light to every man who comes into the world.

He was in the world, and the world was made by Him, and the world did not know Him. He came to His own, and His own did not receive Him. But as many as received Him, to them He gave power to become the sons of God, even to those who believe in His name, who were born, not of blood, nor of the will of the flesh, nor of the will of man, but of God.

## THE INCARNATION

John begins his Gospel with a strong statement about the Incarnation of Jesus (see section 1). This word comes from a Latin term that means "embodied in flesh." Jesus existed before time began as the divine Son of God, and He participated in the creation of the world. But He took on a physical body at His birth into the world to identify with the human race. While He sympathizes with humankind in its weakness, He has the divine power to resist temptation and to deliver earth-bound people from the grip of sin.

And the Word was made flesh and dwelled among us (and we saw His glory, the glory as of the only begotten of the Father), full of grace and truth.

John bore witness of Him and cried, saying, "This was He of whom I spoke, 'He who comes after me is preferred before me, for He was before me.'"

And we have all received of His fullness, and grace for grace. For the law was given by Moses, but grace and truth came by Jesus Christ. No man has seen God at any time. The only begotten Son, who is in the bosom of the Father, He has declared Him. *John 1:1–18*

# 2. THE SUFFERING SERVANT

Who has believed our report? And to whom has the arm of the LORD been revealed?

For He shall grow up before Him as a tender plant, and as a root out of a dry ground. He has no form or splendor, and when we see Him, there is no beauty that we should desire Him.

He was despised and rejected by men, a man of sorrows and acquainted with grief. And we hid, as it were, our faces from Him. He was despised, and we did not esteem Him.

Surely He has borne our griefs and carried our sorrows, yet we considered Him struck, wounded by God and afflicted.

But He was wounded for our transgressions, He was bruised for our iniquities. The chastisement of our peace was on Him, and with His lashes we are healed.

We all like sheep have gone astray. We have turned, each one, to his own way, and the LORD has laid the iniquity of us all on Him.

## "A Lamb to the Slaughter"

He was oppressed and He was afflicted, yet He did not open His mouth. He was brought as a lamb to the slaughter, and as a sheep before its shearers is mute, so He did not open His mouth.

He was taken from prison and from judgment, and who shall declare His generation? For He was cut off out of the land of the living. He was struck for the transgressions of my people.

And He made His grave with the wicked and with the rich in His death because He had done no violence, nor was any deceit in His mouth.

Jesus' death on the cross fulfilled Isaiah's prophecy that He would be a suffering redeemer.

Yet it pleased the LORD to bruise Him. He has put Him to grief. When You make His soul an offering for sin, He shall see His offspring. He shall prolong His days, and the pleasure of the LORD shall prosper in His hand. *Isaiah 53:1–10*

## A SPIRITUAL DELIVERER

About six hundred years before Jesus was born into the world, the prophet Isaiah issued this prophecy about Jesus' life and ministry (see section 2). As the Messiah, Jesus would be totally different from the military champion the Jewish people were expecting. He would come to earth on a redemptive mission, delivering people from their spiritual darkness through His own suffering and death.

Jesus was called the "Son of David,"
a king of Israel known both for
military prowess and musical skill.

# 3. MATTHEW'S GENEALOGY OF JESUS

The book of the generation of Jesus Christ, the son of David, the son of Abraham:

Abraham begot Isaac, and Isaac begot Jacob, and Jacob begot Judah and his brothers.

And Judah begot Perez and Zerah by Tamar, and Perez begot Hezron, and Hezron begot Ram.

And Ram begot Amminadab, and Amminadab begot Nahshon, and Nahshon begot Salmon.

And Salmon begot Boaz by Rahab, and Boaz begot Obed by Ruth, and Obed begot Jesse, and Jesse begot David the king.

And David the king begot Solomon by her who had been the wife of Uriah.

And Solomon begot Rehoboam, and Rehoboam begot Abijah, and Abijah begot Asa.

And Asa begot Jehoshaphat, and Jehoshaphat begot Joram, and Joram begot Uzziah. And Uzziah begot Jotham, and Jotham begot Ahaz, and Ahaz begot Hezekiah.

And Hezekiah begot Manasseh, and Manasseh begot Amon, and Amon begot Josiah. And Josiah begot Jeconiah and his brothers about the time they were carried away to Babylon.

And after they were brought to Babylon, Jeconiah begot Shealtiel, and Shealtiel begot Zerubbabel.

And Zerubbabel begot Abiud, and Abiud begot Eliakim, and Eliakim begot Azor. And Azor begot Zadoc, and Zadoc begot Achim, and Achim begot Eliud.

And Eliud begot Eleazar, and Eleazar begot Matthan, and Matthan begot Jacob.

And Jacob begot Joseph the husband of Mary, of whom was born Jesus, who is called Christ.

## SON OF DAVID

Jesus had no human father, but this genealogy of His human predecessors (see section 3) is the perfect bridge between the Old and New Testaments. Matthew declared that Jesus fulfilled Old Testament prophecy as the Messiah who would be the spiritual heir to the throne of David. Another genealogy of Jesus appears in Luke 3:23–38.

So all the generations from Abraham to David are fourteen generations, and from David until the carrying away into Babylon are fourteen generations, and from the carrying away into Babylon to Christ are fourteen generations. *Matthew 1:1–17*

# 4. A MIRACLE BABY NAMED JOHN

In the days of Herod, the king of Judea, there was a certain priest named Zechariah, of the division of Abijah. And his wife was from the daughters of Aaron, and her name was Elizabeth. And they were both righteous before God, walking blamelessly in all the commandments and ordinances of the Lord. And they had no child, because Elizabeth was barren and they both were now well advanced in years.

And it came to pass, that while he executed the priest's office before God in the order of his division, according to the custom of the priest's office, his lot was to burn incense when he went into the temple of the Lord. And the whole multitude of the people were praying outside at the time of incense. And there an angel of the Lord appeared to him, standing on the right side of the altar of incense. And when Zechariah saw him, he was troubled, and fear fell on him.

### "You Shall Call His Name John"

But the angel said to him, "Do not fear, Zechariah, for your prayer is heard. And your wife, Elizabeth, shall bear you a son, and you shall call his name John. And you shall have joy and gladness, and many shall rejoice at his birth. For he shall be great in the sight of the Lord, and shall drink neither wine nor strong drink.

"And he shall be filled with the Holy Spirit, even from his mother's womb. And he shall turn many of the children of Israel to the Lord their God. And he shall go before Him in the spirit and power of Elijah, to turn the hearts of the fathers to the children, and the disobedient to the wisdom of the just, to make ready a people prepared for the Lord." *Luke 1:5–17*

## 5. ZECHARIAH STRUCK SPEECHLESS

And Zechariah said to the angel, "How shall I know this? For I am an old man, and my wife is well advanced in years."

And the angel answered and said to him, "I am Gabriel, who stands in the presence of God. And I was sent to speak to you and to show you these glad tidings. And behold, you shall be mute and not able to speak until the day that these things shall be performed, because you did not believe my words, which shall be fulfilled in their season."

And the people waited for Zechariah and marveled that he remained so long in the temple. And when he came out, he could not speak to them. And they perceived that he had seen a vision in the temple, for he beckoned to them and remained speechless.

And it came to pass, that as soon as the days of his service were accomplished, he departed to his own house. And after those days his wife, Elizabeth, conceived and hid herself five months, saying, "This is the way the Lord has dealt with me in the days when He looked on me, to take away my reproach among men." *Luke 1:18–25*

## 6. ANNUNCIATION OF JESUS' BIRTH

And in the sixth month the angel Gabriel was sent from God to a city of Galilee named Nazareth, to a virgin betrothed to a man whose name was Joseph, of the house of David. And the virgin's name was Mary. And the angel came in and said to her, "Rejoice, you who are highly favored. The Lord is with you. You are blessed among women."

And when she saw him, she was troubled at his saying and considered what manner of greeting this should be. And the angel said to her, "Do not fear, Mary, for you have found favor with God. And, behold, you shall conceive in your womb and bring forth a Son, and shall call His name Jesus. He shall be great and shall be called the Son of the Highest. And the Lord God shall give to Him the throne of His father David. And He shall reign over the house of Jacob forever, and of His kingdom there shall be no end."

## "How Shall This Be?"

Then Mary said to the angel, "How shall this be, since I do not know a man?"

And the angel answered and said to her, "The Holy Spirit shall come on you, and the power of the Highest shall overshadow you. Therefore, also, the Holy One who shall be born of you shall be called the Son of God. And behold, your cousin Elizabeth, she has also conceived a son in her old age, and this is the sixth month with her who was called barren. For with God nothing shall be impossible."

And Mary said, "Behold the handmaid of the Lord. May it be to me according to your word." And the angel departed from her. *Luke 1:26–38*

The angel Gabriel announces the forthcoming birth of Jesus to Mary.

## 7. MARY VISITS HER COUSIN ELIZABETH

And in those days Mary arose and went in a hurry into the hill country, into a city of Judah, and entered into the house of Zechariah, and greeted Elizabeth. And it came to pass, that when Elizabeth heard the greeting of Mary, the baby leaped in her womb, and Elizabeth was filled with the Holy Spirit.

And she spoke out with a loud voice and said, "You are blessed among women, and the fruit of your womb is blessed. And why has this happened to me, that the mother of my Lord should come to me? For behold, as soon as the voice of your greeting sounded in my ears, the baby in my womb leaped for joy. And blessed is she who believed, for there shall be a fulfillment of those things that were told her from the Lord." *Luke 1:39–45*

### MOTHERS-IN-WAITING

Elizabeth was expecting the baby who became John the Baptist when her cousin Mary came for a visit (see section 7). Mary herself may have been carrying the child Jesus at this time. The two women must have had many discussions about the supernatural events that had made them mothers-to-be. The birth of their miracle babies—Jesus and His forerunner John—would change the world in ways that probably neither of them could fully understand.

## 8. MARY'S SONG OF PRAISE

And Mary said,

> "My soul magnifies the Lord, and my spirit has rejoiced in God my Savior.
> For He has regarded the low estate of His handmaiden. For, behold, from now on all generations shall call me blessed.
> For He who is mighty has done great things for me, and holy is His name.
> And His mercy is on those who fear Him from generation to generation.
> He has shown strength with His arm; He has scattered the proud in the imagination of their hearts.
> He has put down the mighty from their seats and exalted those of low degree.
> He has filled the hungry with good things, and He has sent the rich away empty.
> He has helped His servant Israel, in remembrance of His mercy, as He spoke to our fathers, to Abraham and to his descendants forever."

And Mary remained with her about three months and returned to her own house. *Luke 1:46–56*

## 9. JOHN THE BAPTIST IS BORN

Now Elizabeth's full time came that she should be delivered, and she brought forth a son. And her neighbors and her relatives heard how the Lord had shown great mercy to her, and they rejoiced with her.

And it came to pass, that on the eighth day they came to circumcise the child. And they called him Zechariah, after the name of his father. And his mother answered and said, "Not so, but he shall be called John."

And they said to her, "There is no one of your family who is called by this name." And they made signs to his father, how he would have him called.

And he asked for a writing tablet and wrote, saying, "His name is John." And they all marveled. And immediately his mouth was opened and his tongue released, and he spoke and praised God. And fear came on all who dwelled around them. And all these sayings were widely reported throughout all the hill country of Judea.

And all those who heard them laid them up in their hearts, saying, "What manner of child shall this be?" And the hand of the Lord was with him. *Luke 1:57–66*

## 10. SONG OF ZECHARIAH AT JOHN'S BIRTH

And his father, Zechariah, was filled with the Holy Spirit and prophesied, saying,

"Blessed is the Lord God of Israel, for He has visited and redeemed His people, and has raised up a horn of salvation for us in the house of His servant David, as He spoke by the mouth of His holy prophets, who have been since the world began, that we should be saved from our enemies and from the hand of all who hate us, to perform the mercy promised to our father and to remember His holy covenant, the oath that He swore to our father Abraham, that He would grant to us that we, being delivered out of the hand of our enemies, might serve Him without fear, in holiness and righteousness before Him all the days of our life.

"And you, child, shall be called the prophet of the Highest, for you shall go before the face of the Lord to prepare His ways, to give knowledge of salvation to His people by the remission of their sins, through the tender mercy of our God, with which the Dayspring from on high has visited us, to give light to those who sit in darkness and in the shadow of death, to guide our feet into the way of peace."

And the child grew, and became strong in spirit, and was in the deserts till the day of his appearance to Israel. *Luke 1:67–80*

John the Baptist gazes up at his younger relative Jesus as the baby's mothers, Elizabeth and Mary, look on.

## 11. REASSURANCE FOR JOSEPH

Now the birth of Jesus Christ was in this way: when His mother, Mary, was betrothed to Joseph, before they came together, she was found with child from the Holy Spirit. Then Joseph, her husband, being a just man and not willing to make her a public example, was resolved to put her away secretly.

But while he thought on these things, behold, the angel of the Lord appeared to him in a dream, saying, "Joseph, son of David, do not fear to take to you Mary your wife, for what is conceived in her is from the Holy Spirit. And she shall bring forth a Son, and you shall call His name JESUS, for He shall save His people from their sins."

Now all this was done that it might be fulfilled what was spoken from the Lord by the prophet, saying: "Behold, a virgin shall be with child and shall bring forth a Son, and they shall call His name Immanuel," which being interpreted is "God with us."

Then Joseph, being raised from sleep, did as the angel of the Lord had asked him and took to him his wife, and did not know her till she had brought forth her firstborn Son. And he called His name JESUS. *Matthew 1:18–25*

Joseph ponders what to do about Mary's mysterious pregnancy.

# CHAPTER 2

## Jesus' Birth and His Childhood Years

*Little is known about Jesus during His infancy and boyhood years. The Gospels tell us He was born in Bethlehem, dedicated in the temple in Jerusalem at eight days old, raised in Nazareth, and brought to Jerusalem by His parents as a boy. These brief glimpses set the stage for a life that was fully dedicated to God and the redemptive mission that brought Him into the world.*

## 12. BIRTH OF JESUS IN BETHLEHEM

And it came to pass in those days that there went out a decree from Caesar Augustus that all the world should be registered for a census. (And this census was first made when Quirinius was governor of Syria.) And all went to be registered, everyone to his own city.

And Joseph also went up from Galilee, out of the city of Nazareth, into Judea, to the city of David, which is called Bethlehem, because he was of the house and lineage of David, to be registered with Mary, his betrothed wife, who was great with child.

And so it was, that while they were there, the days were accomplished that she should be delivered. And she brought forth her firstborn son, and wrapped Him in swaddling cloths, and laid Him in a manger, because there was no room for them in the inn. *Luke 2:1–7*

### PROPHECY FULFILLED

An order from the Roman government required all Jewish citizens to register for taxation purposes in their ancestral city (see section 12). The prophet Micah had predicted many years before that the Messiah would be born in the village of Bethlehem (Micah 5:2). It was known as the "city of David" because of its association with King David in his early years.

## 13. SHEPHERDS HEAR THE GOOD NEWS

And in the same country there were shepherds abiding in the field, keeping watch over their flock by night. And, behold, the angel of the Lord came to them, and the glory of the Lord shone around them, and they were greatly afraid.

And the angel said to them, "Do not fear, for behold, I bring you good tidings of great joy, which shall be to all people. For to you is born this day in the city of David a Savior, who is Christ the Lord. And this shall be a sign to you: you shall find the baby wrapped in swaddling cloths, lying in a manger." And suddenly with the angel there was a multitude of the heavenly host praising God and saying, "Glory to God in the highest, and on earth peace, goodwill toward men."

And it came to pass, as the angels had gone away from them into heaven, the shepherds said to one another, "Let us now go even to Bethlehem and see this thing that has come to pass, which the Lord has made known to us."

And they came in a hurry and found Mary and Joseph, and the baby lying in a manger. And when they had seen Him, they widely made known the saying that was told them concerning this Child. And all those who heard it wondered at those things that were told them by the shepherds. But Mary kept all these things and pondered them in her heart.

And the shepherds returned, glorifying and praising God for all the things that they had heard and seen, as it was told to them. *Luke 2:8–20*

Shepherds visit the baby Jesus and His parents soon after He was born.

# 14. DEDICATION OF JESUS IN THE TEMPLE

And when eight days were accomplished for the circumcising of the child, His name was called JESUS, which was so named by the angel before He was conceived in the womb.

And when the days of her [Mary's] purification according to the law of Moses were accomplished, they brought Him to Jerusalem to present Him to the Lord (as it is written in the law of the Lord, "Every male who opens the womb shall be called holy to the Lord") and to offer a sacrifice according to what is said in the law of the Lord: "a pair of turtledoves or two young pigeons."

## Simeon's Testimony

And behold, in Jerusalem there was a man whose name was Simeon, and the same man was just and devout, waiting for the consolation of Israel, and the Holy Spirit was on him. And it was revealed to him by the Holy Spirit that he should not see

Simeon recognizes the infant Jesus as the promised Messiah.

death before he had seen the Lord's Christ. And he came by the Spirit into the temple. And when the parents brought in the Child Jesus, to do for Him according to the custom of the law, then he took Him up in his arms and blessed God and said,

Lord, now You are letting Your servant depart in peace, according to Your word.
For my eyes have seen Your salvation that You have prepared before the face of all peoples,
A light to lighten the Gentiles, and the glory of Your people Israel.

And Joseph and His mother marveled at those things that were spoken of Him. And Simeon blessed them and said to Mary, His mother, "Behold, this Child is set for the fall and rising again of many in Israel, and for a sign that shall be spoken against (yes, a sword shall pierce through your own soul also), that the thoughts of many hearts may be revealed."

## Anna's Thanksgiving

And there was Anna, a prophetess, the daughter of Phanuel, of the tribe of Asher. She was of a great age and had lived with a husband seven years from her virginity. And she was a widow of about eighty-four years, who did not depart from the temple but served God with fasting and prayer night and day. And coming in that instant she likewise gave thanks to the Lord and spoke of Him to all those who looked for redemption in Jerusalem. *Luke 2:21–38*

# 15. WISE MEN SEEK THE NEWBORN KING

Now when Jesus was born in Bethlehem of Judea in the days of Herod the king, behold, there came wise men from the east to Jerusalem, saying, "Where is He who is born King of the Jews? For we have seen His star in the East and have come to worship Him."

When Herod the king had heard these things, he was troubled, and all Jerusalem with him. And when he had gathered all the chief priests and scribes of the people together, he demanded of them where Christ should be born.

And they said to him, "In Bethlehem of Judea, for this is what is written by the prophet: 'And you, Bethlehem, in the land of Judah, are not the least among the princes of Judah. For out of you shall come a Governor who shall rule My people Israel.'" *Matthew 2:1–6*

## A DELAYED VISIT?

A period of about two years may have elapsed between the time of Jesus' presentation in the temple and the arrival of the wise men in Bethlehem (see section 15). Matthew's account says they came "into the house" where Jesus and His parents lived (Matthew 2:11). And Herod slaughtered young children near Bethlehem who were "two years old and under" in an attempt to kill the infant Jesus.

Wise men travel to pay homage to the "King of the Jews."

## 16. GIFTS PRESENTED TO JESUS

Then Herod, when he had secretly called the wise men, diligently inquired of them what time the star appeared. And he sent them to Bethlehem and said, "Go and search diligently for the young Child, and when you have found Him, bring me word again, that I may come and worship Him also."

When they had heard the king, they departed. And behold, the star that they saw in the East went before them, till it came and stood over where the young Child was. When they saw the star, they rejoiced with exceedingly great joy. And when they had come into the house, they saw the young Child with Mary, His mother, and fell down and worshipped Him. And when they had opened their treasures, they presented gifts to Him: gold, and frankincense, and myrrh.

And being warned by God in a dream that they should not return to Herod, they departed to their own country another way. *Matthew 2:7–12*

# 17. THE FLIGHT INTO EGYPT

And when they [the wise men] had departed, behold, the angel of the Lord appeared to Joseph in a dream, saying, "Arise, and take the young Child and His mother, and flee into Egypt, and stay there until I bring you word, for Herod will seek the young Child to destroy Him."

When he [Joseph] arose, he took the young Child and His mother by night and departed into Egypt, and was there until the death of Herod, that it might be fulfilled what was spoken from the Lord by the prophet, saying, "Out of Egypt I have called My Son." *Matthew 2:13–15*

Joseph prepares to lead his family out of harm's way, immediately obeying an angel's command to travel to Egypt.

# 18. HEROD SLAUGHTERS INNOCENT CHILDREN

Then Herod, when he saw that he was mocked by the wise men, was exceedingly angry and sent forth and slew all the children who were in Bethlehem and in all its surrounding area, from two years old and under, according to the time that he had diligently inquired of the wise men.

Then it was fulfilled what was spoken by Jeremiah the prophet, saying: "A voice was heard in Ramah, lamentation and weeping, and great mourning, Rachel weeping for her children, and would not be comforted, because they are no more." *Matthew 2:16–18*

## HEROD THE CRUEL

This killing campaign (see section 18) was in keeping with Herod the Great's reputation as a power-hungry tyrant. He feared this newborn "King of the Jews" would grow up to challenge his power as the supreme ruler over the Jewish people. His paranoia also led him to order members of his own family killed to eliminate any possible threats to his rule.

# 19. JESUS AT HOME IN NAZARETH

But when Herod was dead, behold, an angel of the Lord appeared in a dream to Joseph in Egypt, saying, "Arise, and take the young Child and His mother, and go into the land of Israel, for those who sought the young Child's life are dead."

And he arose, and took the young Child and His mother, and came into the land of Israel. But when he heard that Archelaus was reigning in Judea in place of his father, Herod, he was afraid to go there. However, being warned by God in a dream, he turned aside into the parts of Galilee. And he came and dwelled in a city called Nazareth, that it might be fulfilled what was spoken by the prophets: "He shall be called a Nazarene." *Matthew 2:19–23*

SEE PARALLEL ACCOUNT AT LUKE 2:39–40

# 20. A BOY AMONG THE SCHOLARS

Now His [Jesus'] parents went to Jerusalem every year at the Feast of the Passover. And when He was twelve years old, they went up to Jerusalem according to the custom of the feast. And when they had fulfilled the days, as they returned, the Child Jesus remained behind in Jerusalem. And Joseph and His mother did not know of it.

But they, supposing Him to have been in the company, went a day's journey, and they sought Him among their relatives and acquaintances. And when they

The boy Jesus talks with Jewish teachers in Jerusalem.

did not find Him, they turned back again to Jerusalem, seeking Him. And it came to pass that after three days they found Him in the temple, sitting in the midst of the teachers, both hearing them and asking them questions. And all who heard Him were astonished at His understanding and answers.

And when they saw Him, they were amazed. And His mother said to Him, "Son, why have You dealt with us in this way? Behold, Your father and I have sought You sorrowing."

And He said to them, "How is it that you sought Me? Did you not know that I must be about My Father's business?" And they did not understand the saying that He spoke to them. And He went down with them, and came to Nazareth, and was obedient to them, but His mother kept all these sayings in her heart.

And Jesus increased in wisdom and stature, and in favor with God and man.
*Luke 2:41–52*

# CHAPTER 3

## Jesus Launches His Ministry in Judea and Samaria

*This region in southern Palestine is where Jesus' forerunner, John the Baptist, was preaching. After His baptism by John, Jesus also spent several months in this territory. He did make one trip north during this time into Galilee, where He performed His first miracle.*

# 21. JOHN THE BAPTIST PREPARES THE WAY

Now in the fifteenth year of the reign of Tiberius Caesar, Pontius Pilate being governor of Judea, and Herod being tetrarch of Galilee, and his brother Philip tetrarch of Iturea and of the region of Trachonitis, and Lysanias the tetrarch of Abilene, Annas and Caiaphas being the high priests, the word of God came to John the son of Zechariah in the wilderness. And he came into all the country around the Jordan, preaching the baptism of repentance for the remission of sins, as it is written in the book of the words of Isaiah the prophet, saying:

> The voice of one crying in the wilderness: "Prepare the way of the Lord; make His paths straight.
>
> Every valley shall be filled, and every mountain and hill shall be brought low.
>
> And the crooked shall be made straight, and the rough ways shall be made smooth.
>
> And all flesh shall see the salvation of God."

## "Fruit Worthy of Repentance"

Then he said to the multitude that came forth to be baptized by him, "O generation of vipers, who has warned you to flee from the wrath to come? Therefore bring forth fruit worthy of repentance, and do not begin to say within yourselves, 'We have Abraham as our father.' For I say to you that God is able to raise up children for Abraham from these stones. And also now the axe is laid to the root of the trees. Therefore every tree that does not bring forth good fruit is cut down and cast into the fire."

And the people asked him, saying, "What shall we do then?"

He answered and said to them, "He who has two coats, let him give to him who has none. And he who has food, let him do likewise."

Then tax collectors also came to be baptized and said to him, "Master, what shall we do?"

And he said to them, "Collect no more than what is appointed for you."

And the soldiers likewise demanded of him, saying, "And what shall we do?"

And he said to them, "Do not do violence to any man, and do not accuse anyone falsely. And be content with your wages."

## JOHN THE PROPHET

Other accounts of John the Baptist and his preaching (see section 21) appear in Matthew 3:1–12 and Mark 1:1–8. These two Gospels tell us that John wore clothing made of camel's hair and ate locusts and wild honey. This symbolized his identification with the prophets of the Old Testament, particularly Elijah (see 2 Kings 1:8).

John the Baptist urges people to get ready for the revolutionary ministry of Jesus.

Jesus submits to baptism by John the Baptist.

### "One Mightier than I Is Coming"

And as the people were in expectation, and all men mused in their hearts about John, whether he was the Christ or not, John answered, saying to them all, "Indeed I baptize you with water, but One mightier than I is coming, the strap of whose shoes I am not worthy to untie. He shall baptize you with the Holy Spirit and with fire. His fan is in His hand, and He will thoroughly purge His floor and will gather the wheat into His storehouse. But He will burn the chaff with unquenchable fire."

And he preached to the people many other things in his exhortation. *Luke 3:1–18*

## 22. JOHN BAPTIZES JESUS

Then Jesus came from Galilee to the Jordan to John to be baptized by him. But John forbade Him, saying, "I have need to be baptized by You, and are You coming to me?"

And Jesus, answering, said to him, "Allow it to be so now, for thus it becomes us to fulfill all righteousness." Then he allowed Him.

And when He was baptized, Jesus went up immediately out of the water. And behold, the heavens were opened to Him, and He saw the Spirit of God descending like a dove and lighting on Him. And behold, a voice from heaven said, "This is My beloved Son, in whom I am well pleased." *Matthew 3:13–17*

### A MINISTRY LAUNCHED

Jesus' baptism by John (see section 22) marks the beginning of His ministry. While He was sinless and had no need to repent, He identified through His baptism with John's message. Accounts of His baptism also appear in Mark 1:9–11 and Luke 3:21–23. Luke noted that Jesus was about thirty years old at the time.

## 23. VICTORY OVER SATAN'S TEMPTATIONS

And Jesus, being full of the Holy Spirit, returned from the Jordan and was led by the Spirit into the wilderness, being tempted for forty days by the devil. And in those days He ate nothing. And after they had ended, He was hungry.

And the devil said to Him, "If You are the Son of God, command this stone to be made bread."

And Jesus answered him, saying, "It is written, 'Man shall not live by bread alone, but by every word of God.'"

And the devil, taking Him up to a high mountain, showed to Him all the kingdoms of the world in a moment of time. And the devil said to Him, "I will give You all this power, and their glory. For it is delivered to me and to whomever I will I give it. Therefore, if You will worship me, all this shall be Yours."

### "Get Behind Me, Satan"

And Jesus answered and said to him, "Get behind Me, Satan. For it is written, 'You shall worship the Lord your God, and you shall serve Him only.'"

And he brought Him to Jerusalem, and set Him on a pinnacle of the temple, and said to Him, "If You are the Son of God, cast Yourself down from here. For it is written: 'He shall give His angels charge over You, to guard You,' and, 'In their hands they shall lift You up, lest at any time You dash your foot against a stone.'"

And Jesus answered and said to him, "It is said, 'You shall not tempt the Lord your God.'"

And when the devil had ended all the temptation, he departed from Him for a season. *Luke 4:1–13*

Jesus among animals in the wilderness, according to Mark's Gospel.

## 24. JESUS AS THE LAMB OF GOD

And this is the record of John, when the Jews sent priests and Levites from Jerusalem to ask him, "Who are you?"

And he confessed, and did not deny, but confessed, "I am not the Christ."

And they asked him, "What then? Are you Elijah?"

And he said, "I am not."

"Are you the Prophet?"

And he answered, "No."

Then they said to him, "Who are you, that we may give an answer to those who sent us? What do you say about yourself?"

### "Make Straight the Way of the Lord"

He said, "I am 'the voice of one crying in the wilderness: "Make straight the way of the Lord,"' as the prophet Isaiah said."

And those who were sent were of the Pharisees. And they asked him and said to him, "Why then do you baptize, if you are not the Christ, nor Elijah, nor the Prophet?"

John answered them, saying, "I baptize with water, but there stands One among you, whom you do not know. It is He who, coming after me, is preferred before me, whose shoe strap I am not worthy to untie." These things were done in Bethany beyond the Jordan, where John was baptizing.

The next day John saw Jesus coming to him and said, "Behold, the Lamb of God who takes away the sin of the world. This is He of whom I said, 'After me comes a Man who is preferred before me, for He was before me.' And I did not know Him, but I came baptizing with water so that He would be revealed to Israel."

And John bore witness, saying, "I saw the Spirit descending from heaven like a dove, and it remained on Him. And I did not know Him, but He who sent me to baptize with water, the same said to me, 'On whom you shall see the Spirit descending, and remaining on Him, He is the same who baptizes with the Holy Spirit.' And I saw and bore witness that this is the Son of God." *John 1:19–34*

## 25. JESUS MEETS HIS FIRST DISCIPLES

Again, the next day John stood with two of his disciples, and looking at Jesus as He walked, he said, "Behold, the Lamb of God!" And the two disciples heard him speak, and they followed Jesus.

Then Jesus turned and saw them following and said to them, "What do you seek?"

They said to Him, "Rabbi" (which is to say, being interpreted, Master), "where do You dwell?"

He said to them, "Come and see." They came and saw where He dwelled and

Simon Peter marvels when Jesus identifies him as Cephas, or "a stone."

stayed with Him that day, for it was about the tenth hour.

One of the two who heard John speak and followed Him was Andrew, Simon Peter's brother. He first found his own brother Simon and said to him, "We have found the Messiah," which is, being interpreted, the Christ.

### "You Shall Be Called Cephas"

And he brought him to Jesus. And when Jesus saw him, He said, "You are Simon the son of John. You shall be called Cephas" (which is by interpretation, A Stone).

The following day Jesus wanted to go forth into Galilee, and found Philip, and said to him, "Follow Me." Now Philip was from Bethsaida, the city of Andrew and Peter.

Philip found Nathanael and said to him, "We have found Him of whom Moses in the Law, and the prophets, wrote, Jesus of Nazareth, the son of Joseph."

And Nathanael said to him, "Can any good thing come out of Nazareth?"

Philip said to him, "Come and see."

Jesus saw Nathanael coming to Him and said of him, "Behold an Israelite indeed, in whom is no deceit!"

Nathanael said to Him, "How do You know me?"

Jesus answered and said to him, "Before Philip called you, when you were under the fig tree, I saw you."

## CURIOSITY SATISFIED

John's identification of Jesus as the Lamb of God (see section 25) aroused the curiosity of two of John's followers—Andrew and a second unknown disciple. After Jesus talked with these two men, Andrew brought his brother Simon Peter to meet Jesus. Then Jesus found Philip and Nathanael and enlisted them as His followers.

These four were apparently the first whom Jesus called as His disciples. Later, Andrew and Peter left their vocation as fishermen to follow Jesus. He may have "tested the waters" with Andrew and Peter on this occasion before calling them later to total commitment (see section 34).

### "You Are the King of Israel"

Nathanael answered and said to Him, "Rabbi, You are the Son of God. You are the King of Israel."

Jesus answered and said to him, "Because I said to you, 'I saw you under the fig tree,' do you believe? You shall see greater things than these." And He said to him, "Truly, truly, I say to you, hereafter you shall see heaven open and the angels of God ascending and descending on the Son of Man." *John 1:35–51*

Jesus and His mother at a wedding feast in Cana of Galilee.

## 26. WATER TURNED INTO WINE

And the third day there was a wedding in Cana of Galilee, and the mother of Jesus was there. And both Jesus and His disciples were called to the wedding. And when they lacked wine, the mother of Jesus said to Him, "They have no wine."

Jesus said to her, "Woman, what have I to do with you? My hour has not yet come."

His mother said to the servants, "Whatever He says to you, do it."

And there were set there six waterpots of stone, according to the manner of the purifying of the Jews, containing two or three firkins apiece. Jesus said to them, "Fill the waterpots with water." And they filled them up to the brim. And He said to them, "Draw some out now, and take it to the master of the feast." And they took it.

When the master of the feast had tasted the water that was made wine and did not know where it was from (but the servants who drew the water knew), the master of the feast called the bridegroom and said to him, "Every man at the beginning sets out good wine, and when men have well drunk, then what is worse. But you have kept the good wine until now."

This beginning of miracles Jesus did in Cana of Galilee and revealed His glory. And His disciples believed in Him. *John 2:1–11*

## 27. NO PLACE FOR BUYING AND SELLING

And the Jews' Passover was at hand, and Jesus went up to Jerusalem. And He found in the temple those who sold oxen and sheep and doves, and the money changers sitting. And when He had made a whip of small cords, He drove them all out of the temple, and the sheep and the oxen, and poured out the changers' money and overturned the tables. And He said to those who sold doves, "Take these things from here. Do not make My Father's house a house of business."

And His disciples remembered that it was written, "The zeal for Your house has eaten Me up."

Then the Jews answered and said to Him, "What sign do You show to us, seeing that You do these things?"

Jesus answered and said to them, "Destroy this temple, and in three days I will raise it up."

Then the Jews said, "It has taken forty-six years to build this temple, and You will raise it up in three days?" But He spoke of the temple of His body. Therefore, when He had risen from the dead, His disciples remembered that He had said this to them, and they believed the scripture and the word that Jesus had said. *John 2:13–22*

## TWO TEMPLE CLEANSINGS?

The other Gospel writers place Jesus' cleansing of the temple (see section 27) near the end of His earthly ministry (see section 176). Did Jesus drive out the merchants a second time, or did John's Gospel place this event at the beginning of His ministry? There is no clear answer to this question. If a second cleansing was needed, the commercialization of the temple must have been a continuing problem that taxed Jesus' patience.

## 28. NICODEMUS AND THE NEW BIRTH

There was a man of the Pharisees named Nicodemus, a ruler of the Jews. The same came to Jesus by night and said to Him, "Rabbi, we know that You are a teacher come from God. For no man can do these miracles that You do unless God is with him."

Jesus answered and said to him, "Truly, truly, I say to you, unless a man is born again, he cannot see the kingdom of God."

Nicodemus said to Him, "How can a man be born when he is old? Can he enter a second time into his mother's womb and be born?"

## "You Must Be Born Again"

Jesus answered, "Truly, truly, I say to you, unless a man is born of water and of the Spirit, he cannot enter into the kingdom of God. What is born of the flesh is flesh, and what is born of the Spirit is spirit. Do not marvel that I said to you, 'You must be born again.' The wind blows where it wishes, and you hear the sound of it but cannot tell where it comes from and where it goes. So is everyone who is born of the Spirit."

Nicodemus answered and said to Him, "How can these things be?"

Jesus answered and said to him, "Are you a master of Israel and do not know these things? Truly, truly, I say to you, we speak of what we do know and testify of what we have seen, and you do not receive our testimony. If I have told you earthly things and you do not believe, how shall you believe if I tell you of heavenly things?

## "The Son of Man Must Be Lifted Up"

"And no man has ascended up to heaven but He who came down from heaven, even the Son of Man who is in heaven. And as Moses lifted up the serpent in the wilderness, even so the Son of Man must be lifted up, that whoever believes in Him should not perish but have eternal life.

"For God so loved the world that He gave His only begotten Son, that whoever believes in Him should not perish but have everlasting life. For God did not send His Son into the world to condemn the world but that the world might be saved through Him.

"He who believes in Him is not condemned, but he who does not believe is condemned already because he has not believed in the name of the only begotten Son of God." *John 3:1–18*

# 29. JOHN FOCUSES ATTENTION ON JESUS

After these things Jesus and His disciples came into the land of Judea, and there He remained with them and baptized. And John was also baptizing in Aenon near to Salim, because there was much water there. And they came and were baptized. For John was not yet cast into prison.

Then there arose a question between some of John's disciples and the Jews about purifying. And they came to John and said to him, "Rabbi, He who was with you beyond the Jordan, to whom you bore witness—behold, the same baptizes, and all men are coming to Him."

John answered and said, "A man can receive nothing except what is given him from heaven. You yourselves bear me witness, that I said, 'I am not the Christ,' but that 'I have been sent before Him.' He who has the bride is the bridegroom. But the friend of the bridegroom, who stands and hears him, rejoices greatly because of the bridegroom's voice. Therefore this joy of mine is fulfilled. He must increase, but I must decrease." *John 3:22–30*

John the Baptist assures the crowds, "I am not the Christ."

## 30. A SURPRISED WOMAN AT A WELL

Therefore, when the Lord knew how the Pharisees had heard that Jesus made and baptized more disciples than John (though Jesus Himself did not baptize, but His disciples), He left Judea and departed again into Galilee.

And He needed to go through Samaria. Then He came to a city of Samaria that is called Sychar, near the parcel of ground that Jacob gave to his son Joseph. Now Jacob's well was there. Jesus therefore, being wearied with His journey, sat there by the well. And it was about the sixth hour. A woman of Samaria came to draw water. Jesus said to her, "Give Me a drink." (For His disciples had gone away to the city to buy food.)

### "How Is It that You. . .Ask for a Drink from Me?"

Then the woman of Samaria said to Him, "How is it that You, being a Jew, ask for a drink from me, a woman of Samaria?" For the Jews have no dealings with the Samaritans.

Jesus answered and said to her, "If you knew the gift of God, and who it is who says to you, 'Give Me a drink,' you would have asked Him, and He would have given you living water."

The woman said to Him, "Sir, You have nothing to draw with, and the well is deep. From where then do You get that living water? Are You greater than our father Jacob, who gave us the well and drank from it himself, and his children and his cattle?"

Jesus answered and said to her, "Whoever drinks of this water shall thirst again, but whoever drinks of the water that I shall give him shall never thirst. But the water that I shall give him shall be in him a well of water springing up into everlasting life."

The woman said to Him, "Sir, give me this water, that I may not thirst, nor come here to draw."

Jesus said to her, "Go, call your husband and come here."

The woman answered and said, "I have no husband."

## "What You Have Said Is True"

Jesus said to her, "You have correctly said, 'I have no husband,' for you have had five husbands, and he whom you now have is not your husband. What you have said is true."

The woman said to Him, "Sir, I perceive that You are a prophet. Our fathers worshipped on this mountain, and You say that in Jerusalem is the place where men ought to worship."

Jesus said to her, "Woman, believe Me, the hour is coming when you shall worship the Father neither on this mountain nor in Jerusalem. You worship what you do not know. We know what we worship, for salvation is of the Jews. But the hour is coming, and now has come, when the true worshippers shall worship the Father in spirit and in truth. For the Father seeks such to worship Him. God is a Spirit, and those who worship Him must worship Him in spirit and in truth."

The woman said to Him, "I know that Messiah (who is called Christ) is coming. When He comes, He will tell us all things."

## "I Who Speak to You Am He"

Jesus said to her, "I who speak to you am He."

And just then His disciples came and marveled that He talked with the woman. Yet no man said, "What do You seek?" or "Why are You talking with her?"

## JESUS IN SAMARIA

The province of Samaria (see section 30) was sandwiched between Judea and Galilee—the two other major regions of the Jewish nation. Samaria was populated by people whom the Jews despised as half-breeds because they had intermarried with Gentiles.

Most full-blooded Jews avoided this area because they considered it unclean. But Jesus deliberately went through Samaria and talked with this sinful woman, signifying that no one was beyond God's love.

Jesus invites a Samaritan woman to drink the "living water" that only He can offer.

The woman then left her waterpot, and went her way into the city, and said to the men, "Come, see a man who told me all things that I ever did. Is this not the Christ?" Then they went out of the city and came to Him. *John 4:1–30*

And many of the Samaritans of that city believed in Him because of the saying of the woman who testified, "He told me all that I ever did." So when the Samaritans had come to Him, they begged Him to remain with them, and He stayed there two days.

And many more believed because of His own word and said to the woman, "Now we believe, not because of your saying, for we ourselves have heard Him and know that this is indeed the Christ, the Savior of the world." *John 4:39–42*

# CHAPTER 4

## Jesus' Early Ministry in the Region of Galilee

*After a brief time in Judea, Jesus began teaching and healing in the province of Galilee, the same territory where He grew up. This region was called "Galilee of the Gentiles" because many non-Jews lived here. Jesus worked in Galilee for about eighteen months. This chapter covers the early events of His Galilean ministry.*

And He [Jesus] came to Nazareth, where He had been brought up. And as His custom was, He went into the synagogue on the Sabbath day and stood up to read. And there was delivered to Him the book of the prophet Isaiah.

And when He had opened the book, He found the place where it was written, "The Spirit of the Lord is upon Me, because He has anointed Me to preach the gospel to the poor. He has sent Me to heal the brokenhearted, to preach deliverance to the captives, and recovery of sight to the blind, to set at liberty those who are bruised, to preach the acceptable year of the Lord."

And He closed the book, and He gave it again to the minister and sat down. And the eyes of all those who were in the synagogue were fastened on Him. And He began to say to them, "Today this scripture is fulfilled in your ears." *Luke 4:16–21*

In His hometown synagogue, Jesus identifies Himself as the promised Messiah.

## A FAMILIAR PASSAGE

In His hometown of Nazareth (see section 31), Jesus read from Isaiah 61:1–2, one of the prophet's "suffering servant" passages that described God's righteous servant who would endure great pain on behalf of His people (see section 2). Jesus declared that the Lord had chosen Him to carry out this mission.

# 32. REJECTED AT NAZARETH, JESUS MOVES TO CAPERNAUM

And all [citizens of Nazareth] bore Him [Jesus] witness and wondered at the gracious words that proceeded out of His mouth. And they said, "Is this not Joseph's son?"

And He said to them, "You will surely say this proverb to Me, 'Physician, heal Yourself. Whatever we have heard done in Capernaum, do also here in Your country.'" And He said, "Truly I say to you, no prophet is accepted in his own country.

"But I tell you the truth, many widows were in Israel in the days of Elijah, when the heavens were shut up three years and six months, when great famine was

Modern Nazareth, successor to the village that Jesus left to take up residence in Capernaum. Some believe this cliff in the foreground is where townspeople tried to "cast Him down headlong."

throughout all the land. But Elijah was sent to none of them, except to Zarephath, a city of Sidon, to a woman who was a widow. And many lepers were in Israel in the time of Elisha the prophet, and none of them was cleansed except Naaman the Syrian."

And when they heard these things, all those in the synagogue were filled with wrath, and rose up and drove Him out of the city, and led Him to the edge of the hill on which their city was built, that they might cast Him down headlong.

But passing through the midst of them, He went His way, and came down to Capernaum, a city of Galilee, and taught them on the Sabbath days. And they were astonished at His doctrine, for His word was with power. *Luke 4:22–32*

## HOPE FOR THE GENTILES

Jesus' neighbors in Nazareth couldn't believe that God loved all people (see section 32). They turned violent when He declared that God had blessed Gentiles in Old Testament times. These included a widow who helped the prophet Elijah (1 Kings 17:9–16) and Naaman, an officer in the Syrian army (2 Kings 5:1–14).

Matthew's parallel account of Jesus' move to Capernaum (Matthew 4:13–16) adds that Jesus' settlement in a region where many Gentiles lived fulfilled Old Testament prophecy. Isaiah had declared that the Messiah would be a light to the Gentiles as well as the Jews (Isaiah 42:6).

## 33. A ROYAL OFFICIAL'S SON HEALED

So Jesus came again into Cana of Galilee, where He made the water wine. And there was a certain nobleman whose son was sick at Capernaum. When he heard that Jesus had come out of Judea into Galilee, he went to Him and begged Him to come down and heal his son, for he was at the point of death. Then Jesus said to him, "Unless you see signs and wonders, you will not believe."

The nobleman said to Him, "Sir, come down before my child dies."

Jesus said to him, "Go your way. Your son lives." And the man believed the word that Jesus had spoken to him, and he went his way. And as he was now going down, his servants met him and told him, saying, "Your son lives."

### HEALING ACROSS THE MILES

This father, whose son was desperately ill (see section 33), was probably an official of the Roman government. Jesus was at Cana, about eighteen miles from the city of Capernaum where the boy and his father lived. Jesus' healing of the boy from that distance shows His unlimited power as well as His compassion for a Gentile family. The "second miracle" cited in this account is the water that Jesus turned into wine at this same village (see section 26).

Then he inquired of them the hour when he began to get better. And they said to him, "Yesterday at the seventh hour the fever left him." So the father knew that it was at the same hour in which Jesus said to him, "Your son lives." And he himself believed, and his whole house.

This again is the second miracle that Jesus did when He had come out of Judea into Galilee. *John 4:46–54*

## 34. FOUR FISHERMEN BECOME DISCIPLES

And it came to pass, that as the people pressed on Him [Jesus] to hear the word of God, He stood by the lake of Gennesaret and saw two ships standing by the lake. But the fishermen had gone out of them and were washing their nets. And He entered into one of the ships, which was Simon's, and asked him to thrust out a little from the land. And He sat down and taught the people out of the ship.

Now when He had finished speaking, He said to Simon, "Launch out into the deep and let down your nets for a catch."

And Simon answered and said to Him, "Master, we have toiled all the night and have taken nothing. Nevertheless, at Your word I will let down the net."

And when they had done this, they caught a great multitude of fish, and their net was breaking. And they beckoned to their partners who were in the other ship, that they should come and help them. And they came and filled both the ships,

Jesus called one third of his twelve disciples—two sets of brothers—from their fishing business on the Sea of Galilee.

## A BORROWED BOAT

Both Matthew (4:18–22) and Mark (1:16–21) contain parallel accounts of the calling of these fishermen (see section 34). But only Luke's Gospel tells us that Jesus borrowed Peter and Andrew's boat and turned it into a pulpit to speak to the crowd. Also, Luke alone includes the account of the miraculous catch of fish and Peter's confession of his own sinfulness. This apparently was not the first time Jesus had invited Andrew and Peter to follow Him (see section 25).

so that they began to sink. When Simon Peter saw it, he fell down at Jesus' knees, saying, "Depart from me, for I am a sinful man, O Lord."

For he and all who were with him were astonished at the catch of the fish that they had taken. And so also were James and John, the sons of Zebedee, who were partners with Simon. And Jesus said to Simon, "Do not fear. From now on you shall catch men." And when they had brought their ships to land, they forsook all and followed Him. *Luke 5:1–11*

## 35. A MAN WITH DEMONS HEALED AT CAPERNAUM

And they [Jesus and His disciples] went into Capernaum, and immediately on the Sabbath day He [Jesus] entered into the synagogue and taught. And they were astonished at His doctrine, for He taught them as one who had authority, and not as the scribes.

And in their synagogue there was a man with an unclean spirit, and he cried out, saying, "Leave us alone. What do we have to do with You, Jesus of Nazareth? Have You come to destroy us? I know who You are—the Holy One of God."

And Jesus rebuked him, saying, "Remain silent, and come out of him." And when the unclean spirit had torn him and cried with a loud voice, he came out of him.

And they were all amazed, to such an extent that they questioned among themselves, saying, "What is this thing? What new doctrine is this? For He commands even the unclean spirits with authority, and they obey Him." And immediately His fame spread everywhere throughout all the region surrounding Galilee. *Mark 1:21–28*

## 36. PETER'S MOTHER-IN-LAW HEALED

And He [Jesus] arose out of the synagogue and entered into Simon's house. And Simon's wife's mother was taken with a great fever, and they begged Him for her. And He stood over her and rebuked the fever, and it left her. And immediately she arose and ministered to them.

Now when the sun was setting, all those who had any sick with various diseases brought them to Him. And He laid His hands on every one of them and healed them. And demons also came out of many, crying out and saying, "You are Christ, the Son of God." And He, rebuking them, did not allow them to speak, for they knew that He was Christ. *Luke 4:38–41*

SEE PARALLEL ACCOUNTS AT MATTHEW 8:14–17 AND MARK 1:29–34

## 37. A MAN HEALED OF LEPROSY

And it came to pass, when He [Jesus] was in a certain city, behold a man who was full of leprosy saw Jesus, fell on his face, and begged Him, saying, "Lord, if You are willing, You can make me clean."

And He put forth His hand and touched him, saying, "I am willing. Be clean." And immediately the leprosy departed from him. And He charged him to tell no man: "But go and show yourself to the priest, and offer for your cleansing as a testimony to them, just as Moses commanded."

But the news about Him spread out even more, and great multitudes came together to hear, and to be healed of their infirmities by Him. And He withdrew Himself into the wilderness and prayed. *Luke 5:12–16*

SEE PARALLEL ACCOUNTS AT MATTHEW 8:2–4 AND MARK 1:40–45

## 38. A LAME MAN HEALED AT CAPERNAUM

And again He [Jesus] entered into Capernaum after some days, and it was reported that He was in the house. And immediately many were gathered together, to such an extent that there was no room to receive them, no, not even around the door. And He preached the word to them.

And they came to Him, bringing one paralytic who was carried by four men. And when they could not come near to Him because of the crowd, they uncovered the roof where He was. And when they had broken it up, they let down the bed on which the paralytic was lying. When Jesus saw their faith, He said to the paralytic, "Son, your sins are forgiven."

But there were some of the scribes sitting there and reasoning in their hearts, "Why does this man speak blasphemies like this? Who can forgive sins but God alone?"

And immediately, when Jesus

Friends lower a disabled man through the roof for healing by Jesus.

Jesus calls
Matthew away
from his tax
collector's table.

perceived in His spirit that they so reasoned within themselves, He said to them, "Why do you reason these things in your hearts? Which is easier, to say to the one who is paralyzed, 'Your sins are forgiven you,' or to say, 'Arise, and take up your bed, and walk'? But so that you may know that the Son of Man has power on earth to forgive sins"—He said to the paralytic—"I say to you, arise, and take up your bed, and go your way to your house."

And immediately he arose, took up the bed, and went out before them all, to such an extent that they were all amazed and glorified God, saying, "We have never seen anything like this." *Mark 2:1–12*

SEE PARALLEL ACCOUNTS AT MATTHEW 9:1–8 AND LUKE 5:17–26

## 39. A TAX COLLECTOR FOLLOWS JESUS

And He [Jesus] went out again by the seaside. And all the multitude came to Him, and He taught them. And as He passed by, He saw Levi [Matthew] the son of Alphaeus sitting at the tax booth and said to him, "Follow Me." And he arose and followed Him. *Mark 2:13–14*

SEE PARALLEL ACCOUNTS AT MATTHEW 9:9 AND LUKE 5:27–28

## 40. JESUS' ASSOCIATION WITH SINNERS

And Levi [Matthew] made Him [Jesus] a great feast in his own house. And there was a great company of tax collectors and of others who sat down with them. But their scribes and Pharisees murmured against His disciples, saying, "Why do you eat and drink with tax collectors and sinners?"

And Jesus answered and said to them, "Those who are healthy do not need a physician, but those who are sick do. I came to call not the righteous but sinners to repentance." *Luke 5:29–32*

SEE PARALLEL ACCOUNTS AT MATTHEW 9:10–13 AND MARK 2:15–17

### A SINNER WITH POTENTIAL

Matthew was one of the publicans, or tax collectors, whom the Jews despised (see section 40). These officials worked with the Roman government to collect the fees that the Jewish people considered burdensome and unjust. But Jesus read Matthew's heart, recognizing that he would make a loyal disciple.

From that point on, Matthew observed Jesus in action and eventually wrote down what he saw. The first Gospel in the New Testament bears the name of this former revenue agent.

Near the end of His earthly ministry, Jesus had a dramatic encounter with another tax collector known as Zacchaeus (see section 170).

## 41. A QUESTION ABOUT FASTING

And they [scribes and Pharisees] said to Him [Jesus], "Why do the disciples of John fast often and make prayers, and likewise the disciples of the Pharisees, but Yours eat and drink?"

And He said to them, "Can you make the children of the bridechamber fast while the bridegroom is with them? But the days will come when the bridegroom shall be taken away from them, and then they shall fast in those days."

And He also spoke a parable to them: "No man puts a piece of a new garment on an old one. Otherwise, both the new will make a tear and the piece that was taken out of the new will not match the old.

"And no man puts new wine into old bottles. Otherwise the new wine will burst the bottles and be spilled, and the bottles shall perish. But new wine must be put into new bottles, and both are preserved. Also no man, having drunk old wine, immediately desires new. For he says, 'The old is better.'" *Luke 5:33–39*

SEE PARALLEL ACCOUNTS AT MATTHEW 9:14–17 AND MARK 2:18–22

## 42. A LAME MAN HEALED AT JERUSALEM

After this there was a feast of the Jews, and Jesus went up to Jerusalem. Now there is in Jerusalem by the sheep market a pool, which is called in the Hebrew tongue Bethesda, having five porches. In these lay a great multitude of sick people—blind, lame, withered—waiting for the moving of the water.

For an angel went down at a certain season into the pool and troubled the water; then whoever stepped in first, after the troubling of the water, was made whole of whatever disease he had. And a certain man was there who had an infirmity thirty-eight years. When Jesus saw him lying there, and knew that he had been now a long time in that condition, He said to him, "Do you want to be healed?"

The sick man answered Him, "Sir, I have no man to put me into the pool when the water is troubled. But while I am coming, another steps down before me."

### "Take Up Your Bed, and Walk"

Jesus said to him, "Rise, take up your bed, and walk."

And immediately the man was healed and took up his bed and walked.

And that day was the Sabbath. Therefore the Jews said to him who was cured, "It is the Sabbath day. It is not lawful for you to carry your bed."

He answered them, "He who healed me, the same said to me, 'Take up your bed and walk.'"

Then they asked him, "Who is the man who said to you, 'Take up your bed and walk'?"

And he who was healed did not know who it was, for Jesus had withdrawn, a

Jesus directs a disabled
man at the Pool of Bethesda
to rise to his feet.

multitude being in that place. Afterward Jesus found him in the temple and said to him, "Behold, you are made whole. Do not sin anymore, lest a worse thing come to you." The man departed and told the Jews that it was Jesus who had healed him. *John 5:1–15*

## 43. JESUS DEFENDS THIS HEALING ON THE SABBATH

And therefore the Jews persecuted Jesus and sought to slay Him, because He had done these things on the Sabbath day. But Jesus answered them, "My Father is working until now, and I work." Therefore the Jews sought all the more to kill Him, because He had not only broken the Sabbath but also said that God was His Father, making Himself equal with God.

Then Jesus answered and said to them, "Truly, truly, I say to you, the Son can do nothing of Himself, but what He sees the Father do. For whatever things He does, the Son likewise also does. For the Father loves the Son and shows Him all things that He does. And He will show Him greater works than these, that you may marvel. For as the Father raises up the dead and gives them life, even so the Son gives life to whom He will.

### "All Men Should Honor the Son"

"For the Father judges no man but has committed all judgment to the Son, that all men should honor the Son even as they honor the Father. He who does not honor the Son does not honor the Father who has sent Him. Truly, truly, I say to you, he who hears My word and believes in Him who sent Me has everlasting life, and shall not come into condemnation but has passed from death to life.

"Truly, truly, I say to you, the hour is coming, and now is, when the dead shall hear the voice of the Son of God. And those who hear shall live. For as the Father has life in Himself, so He has given to the Son to have life in Himself, and has also given Him authority to execute judgment, because He is the Son of Man.

"Do not marvel at this, for the hour is coming in which all who are in the graves shall hear His voice and shall come out—those who have done good, to the resurrection of life, and those who have done evil, to the resurrection of judgment.

### "My Judgment Is Just"

"Of Myself I can do nothing. As I hear, I judge. And My judgment is just, because I do not seek My own will but the will of the Father who has sent Me. If I bear witness of Myself, My witness is not true. There is another who bears witness of Me, and I know that the witness that He witnesses of Me is true.

"You sent to John, and he bore witness to the truth. But I do not receive testimony from man, but I say these things that you might be saved. He was a burning and a shining light, and you were willing for a season to rejoice in his light.

"But I have greater witness than that of John, for the works that the Father has given Me to finish—the same works that I do—bear witness of Me, that the Father has sent Me." *John 5:16–36*

## ACTS OF MERCY

Jesus' healing of a lame man (see section 42) was only one of several miraculous healings He performed on the Sabbath (see sections, 45, 127, 141, and 145). Unlike the legalistic Pharisees, He saw no conflict between the law of Sabbath observance and making people well. Through these acts of mercy and love, He was doing the work of His heavenly Father.

Even the Pharisees admitted that rescuing a trapped animal was not a violation of the prohibition against working on this sacred day. So Jesus told them, "How much better, then, is a man than a sheep? Therefore it is lawful to do good on the Sabbath day" (Matthew 12:12).

This animal rescue operation recalls Jesus' teaching about performing deeds of mercy on the Sabbath.

# 44. CONTROVERSY OVER PICKING GRAIN

At that time Jesus went through the grain on the Sabbath day. And His disciples were hungry and began to pluck the heads of grain and to eat. But when the Pharisees saw it, they said to Him, "Behold, Your disciples are doing what is not lawful to do on the Sabbath day."

But He said to them, "Have you not read what David did when he was hungry, and those who were with him: how he entered into the house of God and ate the showbread, which was not lawful for him to eat, or for those who were with him, but only for the priests? Or have you not read in the Law how on the Sabbath days the priests in the temple profane the Sabbath and are blameless?

"But I say to you that in this place is One greater than the temple. But if you had known what this means, 'I will have mercy and not sacrifice,' you would not have condemned the guiltless. For the Son of Man is Lord even of the Sabbath day." *Matthew 12:1–8*

See parallel accounts at Mark 2:23–28 and Luke 6:1–5

Jesus' disciples, picking a few heads of grain on the Sabbath, draw the ire of the Pharisees.

## 45. A MAN'S PARALYZED HAND HEALED

And it came to pass on another Sabbath, also, that He [Jesus] entered into the synagogue and taught. And there was a man whose right hand was withered. And the scribes and Pharisees watched Him, whether He would heal on the Sabbath day, that they might find an accusation against Him.

But He knew their thoughts and said to the man who had the withered hand, "Rise up and stand forth in the midst." And he arose and stood forth. Then Jesus said to them, "I will ask you one thing: Is it lawful on the Sabbath days to do good or to do evil, to save life or to destroy it?"

And looking around at them all, He said to the man, "Stretch out your hand." And he did so, and his hand was restored healthy as the other. And they were filled with rage and spoke with one another about what they might do to Jesus. *Luke 6:6–11*

SEE PARALLEL ACCOUNTS AT MATTHEW 12:9–14 AND MARK 3:1–6

## 46. JESUS SELECTS THE TWELVE

And it came to pass in those days that He [Jesus] went out to a mountain to pray and continued all night in prayer to God. And when it was day, He called His disciples to Him, and He chose twelve of them whom He also named apostles:

Simon, whom He also named Peter, and Andrew his brother; James and John; Philip and Bartholomew; Matthew and Thomas; James the son of Alphaeus, and Simon called the Zealot; and Judas the brother of James, and Judas Iscariot, who also was the traitor. *Luke 6:12–16*

### THE TWELVE AND THE THREE

Lists of Jesus' disciples (see section 46) also appear in Matthew 10:2–4 and Mark 3:13–19, as well as Acts 1:13. Other names by which some of them are identified are Simon (Peter), Nathanael (Bartholomew), and Didymus or "the twin" (Thomas).

Another Simon is also called "the Zealot" to distinguish him from Simon Peter. A second James is identified as the son of Alphaeus to set him apart from James the brother of John. And another Judas is called the brother of James to distinguish him from Judas Iscariot, who betrayed Jesus.

Of these twelve, three disciples—Peter and the brothers James and John—are mentioned most often in the Gospels.

# CHAPTER 5

## The Sermon on the Mount

*The Sermon on the Mount in Matthew 5–7 is one of the longest discourses of Jesus in the Gospels. He directed it mainly to His disciples in the early phase of His Galilean ministry. The sermon describes the way of life that should characterize those who belong to the kingdom of God. A shorter version of these teaching also appears in Luke 6:17–49. Luke's version is sometimes referred to as the "Sermon on the Plain," because of his statement that Jesus "stood on the plain" as He taught (Luke 6:17). Whatever the place where these principles were delivered, they were revolutionary in their impact*

# 47. A LITANY OF BLESSINGS

And seeing the multitudes, He [Jesus] went up on a mountain, and when He was seated, His disciples came to Him. And He opened His mouth and taught them, saying,

"Blessed are the poor in spirit, for theirs is the kingdom of heaven.

Blessed are those who mourn, for they shall be comforted.

Blessed are the meek, for they shall inherit the earth.

Blessed are those who hunger and thirst after righteousness, for they shall be filled.

Blessed are the merciful, for they shall obtain mercy.

Blessed are the pure in heart, for they shall see God.

Blessed are the peacemakers, for they shall be called the children of God.

Blessed are those who are persecuted for righteousness' sake, for theirs is the kingdom of heaven.

Blessed are you when men revile you and persecute you, and say all manner of evil against you falsely for My sake. Rejoice and be exceedingly glad, for great is your reward in heaven, for so they persecuted the prophets who were before you."
*Matthew 5:1–12*

SEE PARALLEL ACCOUNT AT LUKE 6:20–23

## MOUNT OF BEATITUDES

The place where Jesus delivered His Sermon on the Mount is thought to be on a hillside known today as the Mount of Beatitudes (see section 47). The site is marked by a beautiful little chapel known as the Church of Beatitudes.

# 48. GODLY INFLUENCE IN AN EVIL WORLD

[Jesus said]: "You are the salt of the earth, but if the salt has lost its savor, with what shall it be salted? It is thereafter good for nothing but to be cast out and to be trampled underfoot by men.

"You are the light of the world. A city that is set on a hill cannot be hidden. Nor do men light a candle and put it under a bushel, but on a candlestick, and it gives light to all who are in the house. Let your light so shine before men, that they may see your good works and glorify your Father who is in heaven.

"Do not think that I have come to destroy the Law or the Prophets. I have come not to destroy but to fulfill. For truly I say to you, till heaven and earth pass, one jot or one tittle shall in no way pass from the law, till all is fulfilled. Therefore whoever breaks one of these least commandments, and teaches men so, he shall be called the least in the kingdom of heaven.

"But whoever does and teaches them, the same shall be called great in the kingdom of heaven. For I say to you, that unless your righteousness exceeds the righteousness of the scribes and Pharisees, you shall in no circumstance enter into the kingdom of heaven." *Matthew 5:13–20*

## 49. A NEW STANDARD OF RIGHTEOUSNESS

[Jesus said]: "You have heard that it was said by those of old, 'You shall not kill, and whoever kills shall be in danger of the judgment.' But I say to you that whoever is angry with his brother without a cause shall be in danger of the judgment. And whoever says to his brother, 'Raca,' shall be in danger of the council. But whoever says, 'You fool,' shall be in danger of hellfire.

"Therefore if you bring your gift to the altar, and there remember that your brother has anything against you, leave your gift there before the altar, and go your way. First be reconciled to your brother, and then come and offer your gift.

"Agree with your adversary quickly, while you are on the way with him, lest at any time the adversary deliver you to the judge, and the judge deliver you to the officer, and you be cast into prison. Truly, I say to you, you shall by no means come out from there till you have paid the last farthing.

### "But I Say to You"

"You have heard that it was said by those of old, 'You shall not commit adultery.' But I say to you that whoever looks on a woman to lust after her has already committed adultery with her in his heart. And if your right eye offends you, pluck it out, and cast it from you, for it is profitable for you that one of your members should perish, and not that your whole body should be cast into hell.

"And if your right hand offends you, cut it off and cast it from you, for it is profitable for you that one of your members should perish, and not that your whole body should be cast into hell.

"It has been said, 'Whoever divorces his wife, let him give her a certificate of divorce.' But I say to you that whoever divorces his wife, except for the cause of fornication, causes her to commit adultery. And whoever marries she who is divorced commits adultery.

### "Do Not Swear At All"

"Again you have heard that it has been said by those of old, 'You shall not renounce an oath but perform your oaths to the Lord.' But I say to you, do not swear at all: neither by heaven, for it is God's throne, nor by the earth, for it is His footstool, nor by Jerusalem, for it is the city of the great King.

"Nor shall you swear by your head, because you cannot make one hair white or black. But let your communication be 'Yes, yes' or 'No, no.' For whatever is more than these comes from evil.

"You have heard that it has been said, 'An eye for an eye and a tooth for a tooth.' But I say to you, do not resist evil. But whoever strikes you on your right cheek, turn to him the other also. And if any man sues you in court and takes away your coat, let him have your cloak also. And whoever compels you to go a mile, go with him two. Give to him who asks you, and do not turn away from him who would borrow from you." *Matthew 5:21–42*

SEE PARALLEL ACCOUNT AT LUKE 6:27–30

## 50. TREATING ENEMIES LIKE FRIENDS

[Jesus said]: "You have heard that it has been said, 'You shall love your neighbor and hate your enemy.' But I say to you, love your enemies, bless those who curse you, do good to those who hate you, and pray for those who despitefully use you and persecute you, that you may be the children of your Father who is in heaven. For He makes His sun to rise on the evil and on the good, and sends rain on the just and on the unjust.

Jesus' abuse at the cross was exactly the opposite of His teachings on loving one's enemies.

"For if you love those who love you, what reward do you have? Don't even the tax collectors do the same? And if you greet your brothers only, what do you do more than others? Don't even the tax collectors do so? Therefore you be perfect, even as your Father who is in heaven is perfect." *Matthew 5:43–48*

SEE PARALLEL ACCOUNT AT LUKE 6:32–36

## 51. GOOD DEEDS DONE IN SECRET

[Jesus said]: "Be careful that you do not do your deeds of charity before men, to be seen by them. Otherwise you have no reward from your Father who is in heaven. Therefore when you do your deeds of charity, do not sound a trumpet before you, as the hypocrites do in the synagogues and in the streets, that they may have glory from men. Truly I say to you, they have their reward.

"But when you do deeds of charity, do not let your left hand know what your right hand does, that your deeds of charity may be in secret. And your Father who sees in secret shall Himself reward you openly." *Matthew 6:1–4*

## 52. HOW TO PRAY TO GOD THE FATHER

[Jesus said]: "And when you pray, you shall not be as the hypocrites are. For they love to pray standing in the synagogues and in the corners of the streets, that they may be seen by men. Truly I say to you, they have their reward.

"But you, when you pray, enter into your closet, and when you have shut your door, pray to your Father who is in secret. And your Father who sees in secret shall reward you openly. But when you pray, do not use vain repetitions as the heathen do. For they think that they shall be heard for their many words.

"Therefore do not be like them. For your Father knows what things you have need of before you ask Him. Therefore, pray according to this manner:

"Our Father who is in heaven, hallowed be Your name.
Your kingdom come. Your will be done on earth as it is in heaven.
Give us this day our daily bread.
And forgive us our debts, as we forgive our debtors.
And do not lead us into temptation, but deliver us from evil.
For Yours is the kingdom and the power and the glory forever. Amen.

### THE MODEL PRAYER

This prayer of Jesus (see section 52) also appears in Luke 11:1–4 (section 135). Luke reports that Jesus taught this prayer to His disciples at their request. Luke's version of the prayer does not contain the concluding sentence, "For Yours is the kingdom and the power and the glory forever. Amen."

Jesus often prayed to His Father in quiet, secluded spots.

"For if you forgive men their trespasses, your heavenly Father will also forgive you. But if you do not forgive men their trespasses, your Father will not forgive your trespasses." *Matthew 6:5–15*

## 53. THE RIGHT WAY TO FAST

[Jesus said]: "Moreover, when you fast, do not be like the hypocrites, with a sad face. For they disfigure their faces that they may appear to men to be fasting. Truly I say to you, they have their reward.

"But you, when you fast, anoint your head and wash your face, that you do not appear to men to be fasting, but to your Father who is in secret. And your Father, who sees in secret, shall reward you openly." *Matthew 6:16–18*

## 54. FOCUS ON HEAVENLY TREASURES

[Jesus said]: "Do not lay up for yourselves treasures on earth, where moth and rust corrupt, and where thieves break in and steal. But lay up for yourselves treasures in heaven, where neither moth nor rust corrupts, and where thieves do not break in or steal. For where your treasure is, there your heart will be also.

"The eye is the light of the body. Therefore if your eye is healthy, your whole body shall be full of light. But if your eye is evil, your whole body shall be full of darkness. Therefore if the light that is in you is darkness, how great is that darkness!

### "You Cannot Serve God and Riches"

"No man can serve two masters, for either he will hate the one and love the other, or else he will hold to the one and despise the other. You cannot serve God and riches.

"Therefore I say to you, take no thought for your life, what you shall eat or what you shall drink, or yet for your body, what you shall put on. Isn't life more than food and the body more than clothing? Behold the fowls of the air, for they do not sow; they neither reap nor gather into barns. Yet your heavenly Father feeds them. Aren't you much more valuable than they are? Which of you by worrying can add one cubit to his stature?

"And why do you worry about clothing? Consider the lilies of the field, how they grow: they do not toil, nor do they spin, and yet I say to you that even Solomon in all his glory was not arrayed

### CITIZENS OF GOD'S KINGDOM

Jesus referred often in His teachings to the kingdom of God (see section 54). This kingdom included those who followed Jesus and made their commitment to Him and His teachings the highest priority of their lives. Another phrase that means the same thing is "kingdom of heaven" (see sections 62 and 117).

like one of these. Therefore, if God so clothes the grass of the field, which is here today and tomorrow is cast into the oven, shall He not much more clothe you, O you of little faith?

### "Seek First the Kingdom of God"

"Therefore do not worry, saying, 'What shall we eat?' or 'What shall we drink?' or 'With what shall we be clothed?' For the Gentiles seek after all these things. For your heavenly Father knows that you have need of all these things. But seek first the kingdom of God and His righteousness, and all these things shall be added to you. Therefore don't worry about tomorrow, for tomorrow shall worry about its own things. The day has enough of its own evil." *Matthew 6:19–34*

A lone sparrow recalls Jesus' teachings on God's provision for those who put His kingdom first.

## 55. AVOID HARSH JUDGMENT OF OTHERS

[Jesus said]: "Do not judge, that you not be judged. For with what judgment you judge, you shall be judged. And with what measure you use, it shall be measured to you again.

"And why do you look at the speck that is in your brother's eye but do not consider the beam that is in your own eye? Or how will you say to your brother, 'Let me pull the speck out of your eye,' and behold, a beam is in your own eye? You hypocrite. First cast the beam out of your own eye, and then you shall see clearly to cast the speck out of your brother's eye.

"Do not give what is holy to the dogs. Do not cast your pearls before swine, lest they trample them under their feet and turn back and tear you apart." *Matthew 7:1–6*

SEE PARALLEL ACCOUNT AT LUKE 6:37–38

## 56. TREAT PEOPLE WITH RESPECT

[Jesus said]: "Ask, and it shall be given to you. Seek, and you shall find. Knock, and it shall be opened to you. For everyone who asks receives, and he who seeks finds, and to him who knocks it shall be opened.

"Or what man is there of you who, if his son asks for bread, will give him a stone? Or if he asks for a fish, will give him a serpent? If you then, being evil, know how to give good gifts to your children, how much more shall your Father who is in heaven give good things to those who ask Him? Therefore, in all things, whatever you want men to do to you, you should do just so to them, for this is the Law and the Prophets." *Matthew 7:7–12*

SEE PARALLEL ACCOUNT AT LUKE 6:31

## 57. GOOD DEEDS FLOW FROM A GODLY LIFE

[Jesus said]: "Enter in at the narrow gate, for wide is the gate and broad is the way that leads to destruction, and there are many who go in by it. Because the gate is narrow and the way is narrow that leads to life, and there are few who find it.

"Beware of false prophets, who come to you in sheep's clothing, but inwardly they are ravenous wolves. You shall know them by their fruit. Do men gather grapes from thorns, or figs from thistles? Even so, every good tree brings forth good fruit, but a corrupt tree brings forth evil fruit.

"A good tree cannot bring forth evil fruit, nor can a corrupt tree bring forth good fruit. Every tree that does not bring forth good fruit is cut down and cast into the fire. Therefore by their fruit you shall know them.

"Not everyone who says to Me, 'Lord, Lord,' shall enter into the kingdom of heaven, but he who does the will of my Father who is in heaven. Many will say

### THE GOLDEN RULE

Everyone recognizes Jesus' words at the end of this passage (see section 56) as the Golden Rule. Many other great teachers of the past have cited some version of this principle. For example, the Greek philosopher Socrates stated this rule, but in a negative way: "What stirs your anger when done to you by others, that do not do to them."

By contrast, Jesus stated this principal in positive terms. Citizens of God's kingdom should envision how they want others to treat them, then take the initiative to put this positive treatment into action for others. If practiced, this simple little rule would revolutionize all human relationships.

to Me in that day, 'Lord, Lord, have we not prophesied in Your name, and have cast out demons in Your name, and done many wonderful works in Your name?'

"And then I will profess to them, 'I never knew you. Depart from Me, you who work iniquity.'" *Matthew 7:13–23*

SEE PARALLEL ACCOUNT AT LUKE 6:43–46

Jesus declared that a godly life will bear good works, just as an olive tree will produce fruit of its kind.

## 58. BUILD ON A SOUND FOUNDATION

[Jesus said]: "Therefore whoever hears these sayings of Mine and does them, I will compare him to a wise man who built his house on a rock. And the rain descended, and the floods came, and the winds blew and beat on that house, and it did not fall, for it was founded on a rock.

"And everyone who hears these sayings of Mine and does not do them shall be compared to a foolish man who built his house on the sand. And the rain descended, and the floods came, and the winds blew and beat on that house, and it fell. And great was its fall."

And it came to pass, when Jesus had ended these sayings, the people were astonished at His doctrine, for He taught them as one having authority, and not as the scribes. *Matthew 7:24–29*

# CHAPTER 6

---

## Jesus' Continuing Ministry in the Region of Galilee

*This chapter includes events in the later phase of Jesus' ministry in Galilee. This period brought widespread recognition of His ability as a teacher and healer. But opposition from the Pharisees and other religious leaders grew in direct proportion to His popularity with the common people.*

Jesus brings the son of a grieving widow back to life.

## 59. A CENTURION'S SERVANT HEALED

Now when He [Jesus] had ended all His sayings in the audience of the people, He entered into Capernaum. And a certain centurion's servant, who was dear to him, was sick and ready to die. And when he heard of Jesus, he sent the elders of the Jews to Him, beseeching Him that He would come and heal his servant.

And when they came to Jesus, they begged Him insistently, saying that he for whom He should do this was worthy, "for he loves our nation, and he has built us a synagogue."

Then Jesus went with them. And when He was now not far from the house, the centurion sent friends to Him, saying to Him, "Lord, do not trouble Yourself, for I am not worthy that You should enter under my roof. Therefore I did not think myself worthy to come to You. But say in a word, and my servant shall be healed. For I also am a man set under authority, having soldiers under me. And I say to one, 'Go,' and he goes, and to another, 'Come,' and he comes, and to my servant, 'Do this,' and he does it."

When Jesus heard these things, He marveled at him and turned around and said to the people who followed Him, "I say to you, I have not found so great faith, no, not in Israel." And returning to the house, those who were sent found the servant healed who had been sick. *Luke 7:1–10*

SEE PARALLEL ACCOUNT AT MATTHEW 8:5–13

## 60. A WIDOW'S SON RAISED FROM THE DEAD

And it came to pass the day after, that He [Jesus] went into a city called Nain. And many of His disciples and many people went with Him. Now when He came near the gate of the city, behold, there was a dead man carried out, the only son of his mother, and she was a widow. And many people of the city were with her.

And when the Lord saw her, He had compassion on her and said to her, "Do not weep." And He came and touched the bier, and those who bore him stood still. And He said, "Young man, I say to you, arise." And he who was dead sat up and began to speak. And He delivered him to his mother.

### JESUS' POWER OVER DEATH

The widow's son whom Jesus restored to life (see section 60) is one of three people whom He raised from the dead during His ministry. The other two were the daughter of Jairus (section 87) and His friend Lazarus (section 157).

This miracle at Nain is memorialized by a little church known as the Resurrection of the Widow's Son, built in the 1800s. It stands today in an Arab village known as Kafr-Nin, which preserves the name of the little town.

And there came a fear on all, and they glorified God, saying, "A great prophet has risen up among us" and "God has visited His people." And this rumor of Him went forth throughout all Judea, and throughout all the surrounding region. *Luke 7:11–17*

## 61. JESUS REASSURES JOHN THE BAPTIST

And John, calling to him two of his disciples, sent them to Jesus, saying, "Are You He who should come, or do we look for another?" When the men had come to Him, they said, "John the Baptist has sent us to You, saying, 'Are You He who should come, or do we look for another?'"

And in that same hour He cured many of their infirmities and plagues and evil spirits, and He gave sight to many who were blind.

Then Jesus answered and said to them, "Go your way, and tell John the things you have seen and heard: how the blind see, the lame walk, the lepers are cleansed, the deaf hear, the dead are raised, the gospel is preached to the poor. And blessed is he who shall not stumble because of Me." *Luke 7:19–23*

SEE PARALLEL ACCOUNT AT MATTHEW 11:2–6

A group of Pharisees grumbles about the work of Jesus and John the Baptist.

## 62. JOHN AND THE PROPHET ELIJAH

And as they [disciples of John the Baptist] departed, Jesus began to say to the multitudes concerning John: "What did you go out into the wilderness to see? A reed shaken with the wind? But what did you go out to see? A man clothed in soft clothing? Behold, those who wear soft clothing are in kings' houses.

"But what did you go out to see? A prophet? Yes, I say to you, and more than a prophet. For this is he of whom it is written: 'Behold, I send My messenger before Your face, who shall prepare Your way before You.'

"Truly I say to you, among those who are born of women there has not risen one greater than John the Baptist. However, he who is least in the kingdom of heaven is greater than he.

"And from the days of John the Baptist until now the kingdom of heaven suffers violence, and the violent take it by force. For all the Prophets and the Law prophesied until John. And if you will receive it, this is Elijah who is to come. He who has ears to hear, let him hear." *Matthew 11:7–15*

SEE PARALLEL ACCOUNT AT LUKE 7:24–28

## 63. PHARISEES REJECT JOHN AND JESUS

And all the people who heard Him [Jesus], and the tax collectors, declared God as righteous, being baptized with the baptism of John. But the Pharisees and lawyers rejected the counsel of God against themselves, not being baptized by him.

And the Lord said, "To what then shall I compare the men of this generation, and to what are they like? They are like children sitting in the marketplace and calling to one another, and saying: 'We have piped for you, and you have not danced; we have mourned for you, and you have not wept.'

"For John the Baptist came neither eating bread nor drinking wine, and you say, 'He has a demon.' The Son of Man has come eating and drinking, and you say, 'Behold a gluttonous man and a drunkard, a friend of tax collectors and sinners!' But wisdom is justified by all her children." *Luke 7:29–35*

SEE PARALLEL ACCOUNT AT MATTHEW 11:16–19

## 64. BAD NEWS FOR UNBELIEVING CITIES

Then He [Jesus] began to upbraid the cities in which most of His mighty works were done, because they did not repent: "Woe to you, Chorazin! Woe to you, Bethsaida! For if the mighty works that were done in you had been done in Tyre and Sidon, they would have repented long ago in sackcloth and ashes. But I say to you, it shall be more tolerable for Tyre and Sidon at the day of judgment than for you.

"And you, Capernaum, who are exalted to heaven, shall be brought down to hell. For if the mighty works that have been done in you had been done in Sodom, it would have remained until this day. But I say to you that it shall be more tolerable for the land of Sodom on the day of judgment than for you." *Matthew 11:20–24*

## 65. PEACE FOR THOSE WHO BELIEVE

At that time Jesus answered and said, "I thank You, O Father, Lord of heaven and earth, because You have hidden these things from the wise and prudent and have revealed them to infants. Even so, Father, for so it seemed good in Your sight.

"All things have been delivered to Me by My Father, and no man knows the Son but the Father. Nor does any man know the Father except the Son and he to whom the Son chooses to reveal Him.

"Come to Me, all you who labor and are heavy-laden, and I will give you rest. Take My yoke on you and learn from Me, for I am meek and lowly in heart, and you shall find rest for your souls. For My yoke is easy and My burden is light." *Matthew 11:25–30*

Jesus commends a sinful woman for her act of kindness and devotion.

# 66. ANOINTING BY A SINFUL WOMAN

And one of the Pharisees asked Him [Jesus] to eat with him. And He went into the Pharisee's house and sat down at the table.

And, behold, a woman in the city who was a sinner, when she knew that Jesus sat at the table in the Pharisee's house, brought an alabaster box of ointment, and stood at His feet behind Him weeping, and began to wash His feet with tears, and wiped them with the hair of her head, and kissed His feet, and anointed them with the ointment. *Luke 7:36–38*

## TWO ACTS OF RESPECT

This anointing of Jesus (see section 66) occurred early in His ministry. It was a lavish display of a wayward woman's esteem for Jesus because of His acceptance of sinners. Mary of Bethany performed a second anointing of Jesus as His ministry was drawing to a close (section 173). He interpreted Mary's action as an anointing for His approaching death. Both anointings show the high regard that women had for Jesus because He accepted them so readily.

# 67. PARABLE OF TWO DEBTORS

Now when the Pharisee who had invited Him [Jesus] saw it [the anointing of Jesus], he spoke to himself, saying, "If He were a prophet, this Man would have known who and what manner of woman this is who is touching Him, for she is a sinner."

And Jesus answered and said to him, "Simon, I have something to say to you."

And he said, "Master, say it."

"There was a certain creditor who had two debtors. The one owed five hundred pence, and the other fifty. And when they had nothing to pay, he freely forgave them both. Tell Me, therefore, which of them will love him most?"

Simon answered and said, "I suppose he to whom he forgave most."

And He said to him, "You have judged rightly. And He turned to the woman and said to Simon, "Do you see this woman? I entered into your house. You gave Me no water for My feet, but she has washed My feet with tears and wiped them with the hair of her head. You gave me no kiss, but this woman has not ceased to kiss My feet since the time I came in.

"You did not anoint My head with oil, but this woman has anointed My feet with ointment. Therefore I say to you, her sins, which are many, are forgiven, for she loved much. But to whom little is forgiven, the same loves little." And He said to her, "Your sins are forgiven."

And those who sat at the table with Him began to say to themselves, "Who is this who also forgives sins?"

And He said to the woman, "Your faith has saved you. Go in peace." *Luke 7:39–50*

## 68. JESUS' MIRACLES ATTRIBUTED TO SATAN

Then one was brought to Him [Jesus] who was possessed with a demon, blind, and mute. And He healed him, to such a degree that the blind and mute man both spoke and saw. And all the people were amazed and said, "Isn't this the Son of David?"

But when the Pharisees heard it they said, "This fellow does not cast out demons but by Beelzebub, the prince of the demons."

And Jesus knew their thoughts and said to them, "Every kingdom divided against itself is brought to desolation, and every city or house divided against itself shall not stand. And if Satan casts out Satan, he is divided against himself. How then shall his kingdom stand?

"And if I cast out demons by Beelzebub, by whom do your children cast them out? Therefore they shall be your judges. But if I cast out demons by the Spirit of God, then the kingdom of God has come to you.

"Or else how can one enter into a strong man's house and rob his goods, except he first binds the strong man? And then he will rob his house. He who is not with Me is against Me, and he who does not gather with Me scatters."
*Matthew 12:22–30*

SEE PARALLEL ACCOUNT
AT MARK 3:22–27

### DOES FORGIVENESS HAVE A LIMIT?

One interpretation of the "unforgivable sin" (see sections 68 and 69) is that it refers to the act of attributing the works of God to Satan. Jesus referred to this as "blasphemy" when the Pharisees claimed He was acting as an agent of Satan rather than God the Father.

But another possibility is that it refers to unbelief in general. Those who persistently refuse to accept Jesus Christ as Lord and Savior are trapped in their condition as hopeless sinners. But forgiveness is available—if and when the unbeliever repents, turns from his sin, and accepts Jesus Christ as Lord and Savior.

## 69. THE SIN THAT CAN'T BE FORGIVEN

[Jesus said]: "Therefore I say to you, all kinds of sin and blasphemy shall be forgiven men, but the blasphemy against the Holy Spirit shall not be forgiven men. And whoever speaks a word against the Son of Man, it shall be forgiven him. But whoever speaks against the Holy Spirit, it shall not be forgiven him, either in this world or in the world to come.

"Either make the tree good and its fruit good, or else make the tree corrupt and its fruit corrupt. For the tree is known by its fruit. O generation of vipers, how can you, being evil, speak good things? For the mouth speaks out of the abundance of the heart. A good man out of the good treasure of the heart brings forth good things, and an evil man out of the evil treasure brings forth evil things.

"But I say to you that every idle word that men speak, they shall give account of it on the day of judgment. For by your words you shall be justified, and by your words you shall be condemned." *Matthew 12:31–37*

SEE PARALLEL ACCOUNT AT MARK 3:28–30

## 70. NO MIRACULOUS SIGN

Then some of the scribes and the Pharisees answered, saying, "Master, we want to see a sign from You."

But He [Jesus] answered and said to them, "An evil and adulterous generation seeks after a sign, and no sign shall be given to it but the sign of the prophet Jonah. For as Jonah was three days and three nights in the whale's belly, so shall the Son of Man be three days and three nights in the heart of the earth.

"The men of Nineveh shall rise in judgment with this generation and shall condemn it, because they repented at the preaching of Jonah. And behold, something greater than Jonah is here.

### "Something Greater than Solomon Is Here"

"The queen of the South shall rise up in the judgment with this generation and shall condemn it, for she came from the farthest parts of the earth to hear the wisdom of Solomon. And behold, something greater than Solomon is here.

"When the unclean spirit has gone out of a man, he walks through dry places, seeking rest, and finds none. Then he says, 'I will return to my house from where I came out.' And when he comes, he finds it empty, swept, and garnished.

"Then he goes and takes with him seven other spirits more wicked than himself, and they enter in and dwell there. And the last state of that man is worse than the first. Even so shall it also be with this wicked generation." *Matthew 12:38–45*

## 71. PARABLE OF THE SOWER

And again He [Jesus] began to teach by the seaside. And a great multitude was gathered to Him, so that He entered into a ship and sat in it on the sea. And the whole multitude was on the land by the sea.

And He taught them many things by parables and said to them in His doctrine, "Listen! Behold, a sower went out to sow. And it came to pass, as he sowed, some seed fell by the wayside, and the fowl of the air came and devoured it up.

"And some fell on stony ground, where it did not have much earth, and immediately it sprang up because it had no depth of earth. But when the sun was up, it was scorched, and because it had no root it withered away. And some fell among thorns, and the thorns grew up and choked it, and it yielded no fruit.

"And other seed fell on good ground and yielded fruit that sprang up and increased and brought forth some thirty and some sixty and some a hundred." And He said to them, "He who has ears to hear, let Him hear." *Mark 4:1–9*

SEE PARALLEL ACCOUNTS AT MATTHEW 13:1–9 AND LUKE 8:4–8

In Jesus' parable, a farmer broadcasts seed in a field.

## 72. WHY JESUS TAUGHT WITH PARABLES

And the disciples came and said to Him [Jesus], "Why do You speak to them in parables?"

He answered and said to them, "Because it is given to you to know the mysteries of the kingdom of heaven, but to them it is not given. For whoever has, to him more shall be given, and he shall have abundance. But whoever does not have, even what he has shall be taken away from him. Therefore I speak to them in parables, because seeing they do not see, and hearing they do not hear, nor do they understand. And in them the prophecy of Isaiah is fulfilled, which says:

'By hearing you shall hear and shall not understand, and seeing you shall see and shall not perceive.

'For this people's heart has become thick, and their ears are dull of hearing. And they have closed their eyes, lest at any time they should see with their eyes and hear with their ears, and should understand with their hearts and should be converted, and I should heal them.'

"But blessed are your eyes, for they see, and your ears, for they hear. For truly I say to you that many prophets and righteous men have desired to see what you see, and have not seen them, and to hear what you hear, and have not heard them."
*Matthew 13:10–17*

SEE PARALLEL ACCOUNTS AT MARK 4:11–12 AND LUKE 8:10

### PARABLES OF THE KINGDOM

The parable of the sower is the first of several parables (see section 71) that Jesus told to reveal the meaning of the kingdom of God. This kingdom is God's rule of grace in the hearts of those who acknowledge Him as Lord and Savior. The parable of the mustard seed shows that this kingdom was small and insignificant when it began. But it would eventually grow into a worldwide spiritual force through the faithful witness of Jesus' followers.

## 73. PARABLE OF THE SOWER EXPLAINED

And when He [Jesus] was alone, those who were around Him with the twelve asked Him about the parable. . . . And He said to them, "Do you not understand this parable? And how then will you understand all parables?" *Mark 4:10, 13*

"Now the parable is this: The seed is the word of God. Those by the wayside are those who hear; then the devil comes and takes away the word out of their hearts, lest they should believe and be saved. Those on the rock are those who, when they hear, receive the word with joy, and these have no root; they believe for a while and fall away in time of temptation.

"And those that fell among thorns are those who, when they have heard, go forth and are choked with cares and riches and pleasures of this life, and bring no fruit to perfection.

"But those on the good ground are those who, having heard the word with an honest and good heart, keep it and bring forth fruit with patience." *Luke 8:11–15*

See parallel account at Matthew 13:13–23

## 74. PARABLE OF THE CANDLE

And He [Jesus] said to them [the disciples], "Is a candle brought to be put under a bushel or under a bed and not to be set on a candlestick? For there is nothing hidden that shall not be made clear, nor is anything kept secret but that it should come into view. If any man has ears to hear, let him hear."

And He said to them, "Be careful what you hear: with what measure you measure, it shall be measured to you, and more shall be given to you who hear. For he who has, to him shall be given, and he who does not have, even what he has shall be taken from him." *Mark 4:21–25*

See parallel account at Luke 8:16–18

In Jesus' parable, the slow growth of seed in the ground represented the steady expansion of the kingdom of God.

## 75. PARABLE OF THE SEED GROWING UNSEEN

And He [Jesus] said, "So the kingdom of God is as if a man should cast seed into the ground, and should sleep and rise night and day, and the seed should spring and grow up; he does not know how.

"For the earth brings forth fruit by itself: first the blade, then the head, after that the full grain in the head. But when the fruit is brought forth, immediately he puts in the sickle, because the harvest has come." *Mark 4:26–29*

## 76. PARABLE OF WEEDS AND WHEAT

He [Jesus] presented another parable to them, saying: "The kingdom of heaven is similar to a man who sowed good seed in his field, but while men slept, his enemy came and sowed weeds among the wheat and went his way. But when the blade had sprung up and brought forth fruit, then the weeds also appeared.

"So the servants of the landowner came and said to him, 'Sir, did you not sow good seed in your field? How then does it have weeds?'

"He said to them, 'An enemy has done this.'

"The servants said to him, 'Then do you want us to go and gather them up?'

"But he said, 'No, lest while you gather up the weeds you also root up the wheat with them. Let both grow together until the harvest, and in the time of harvest I will say to the reapers, 'First gather together the weeds and bind them in bundles to burn them, but gather the wheat into my barn.'" *Matthew 13:24–30*

## 77. MEANING OF THE PARABLE OF WEEDS AND WHEAT

Then Jesus sent the multitude away and went into the house. And His disciples came to Him, saying, "Declare to us the parable of the weeds of the field."

He answered and said to them, "He who sows the good seed is the Son of Man. The field is the world, the good seed are the children of the kingdom, but the weeds are the children of the wicked one.

"The enemy who sowed them is the devil, the harvest is the end of the world, and the reapers are the angels. Therefore as the weeds are gathered and burned in the fire, so shall it be in the end of this world. The Son of Man shall send forth His angels, and they shall gather out of His kingdom all things that cause stumbling and those who do iniquity, and shall cast them into a furnace of fire. There shall be wailing and gnashing of teeth.

"Then the righteous shall shine forth as the sun in the kingdom of their Father. Whoever has ears to hear, let him hear." *Matthew 13:36–43*

A foreign plant in a grainfield recalls Jesus' parable about wheat and weeds growing together.

## 78. PARABLE OF THE MUSTARD SEED

And He [Jesus] said, "To what shall we liken the kingdom of God? Or with what comparison shall we compare it? It is similar to a grain of mustard seed, which, when it is sown in the earth, is less than all the seeds that are in the earth.

"But when it is sown, it grows up and becomes greater than all herbs and shoots out great branches, so that the fowl of the air may lodge under its shadow." *Mark 4:30–32*

SEE PARALLEL ACCOUNT AT MATTHEW 13:31–32

## 79. PARABLE OF LEAVEN IN DOUGH

He [Jesus] spoke to them another parable: "The kingdom of heaven is similar to leaven, which a woman took and hid in three measures of flour till the whole was leavened."

All these things Jesus spoke to the multitude in parables. And without a parable He did not speak to them, that it might be fulfilled what was spoken by the prophet, saying, "I will open My mouth in parables; I will utter things that have been kept secret from the foundation of the world." *Matthew 13:33–35*

SEE PARALLEL ACCOUNT AT LUKE 13:20–21

## 80. PARABLES OF A HIDDEN TREASURE AND A PRECIOUS PEARL

[Jesus said]: "Again, the kingdom of heaven is similar to treasure hidden in a field, which a man found and hid. And for joy over it he goes and sells all that he has and buys that field.

"Again, the kingdom of heaven is similar to a merchant seeking fine pearls, who, when he had found one pearl of great price, went and sold all that he had and bought it." *Matthew 13:44–46*

## 81. PARABLE OF A FISHING NET

[Jesus said]: "Again, the kingdom of heaven is similar to a net that was cast into the sea and gathered some of every kind. When it was full, they pulled it to shore and sat down and gathered the good into vessels, but cast the bad away.

"So shall it be at the end of the world. The angels shall come forth and separate the wicked from among the just, and shall cast them into the furnace of fire. There shall be wailing and gnashing of teeth."

Jesus said to them, "Have you understood all these things?"

They say to Him, "Yes, Lord."

Then He said to them, "Therefore every scribe who is instructed in the kingdom of heaven is similar to a man who is a landowner who brings forth out of his treasure new and old things." *Matthew 13:47–52*

A modern fisherman casts a net, a process similar to that used in Jesus' day.

## 82. JESUS CALMS A STORM

And the same day, when the evening came, He [Jesus] said to them [His disciples], "Let us cross over to the other side." And when they had sent away the multitude, they took Him in the ship, just as He was. And other little ships were also with Him.

And a great storm of wind arose, and the waves beat into the ship, so that it was now full. And He was in the rear part of the ship, asleep on a pillow. And they awoke Him and said to Him, "Master, do You not care that we are perishing?"

And He arose and rebuked the wind and said to the sea, "Peace, be still." And the wind ceased and there was a great calm. And He said to them, "Why are you so fearful? How is it that you have no faith?"

And they feared exceedingly and said to one another, "What kind of man is this, that even the wind and the sea obey Him?" *Mark 4:35–41*

SEE PARALLEL ACCOUNTS AT MATTHEW 8:18, 23–27 AND LUKE 8:22–25

Jesus amazes His disciples by calming the treacherous waves of the Sea of Galilee.

## 83. A WILD MAN AMONG THE TOMBS HEALED

And they [Jesus and His disciples] came over to the other side of the sea, into the country of the Gadarenes. And when He came out of the ship, immediately there met Him out of the tombs a man with an unclean spirit, who had his dwelling among the tombs.

And no man could bind him, no, not with chains, because he had often been bound with shackles and chains, and the chains had been plucked apart by him and the shackles broken in pieces. No man could tame him. And always, night and day, he was in the mountains and in the tombs, crying and cutting himself with stones.

### "Come Out of the Man"

But when he saw Jesus far off, he ran and worshipped Him, and cried with a loud voice, and said, "What have I to do with You, Jesus, Son of the Most High God? I solemnly charge You by God that You do not torment me." For He said to him, "Come out of the man, you unclean spirit!"

And He asked him, "What is your name?"

And he answered, saying, "My name is Legion, for we are many." And he begged Him much that He would not send them away out of the country. Now there was a great herd of swine feeding

Demons cast out of a wild man enter a herd of pigs that drown in the Sea of Galilee.

near the mountains. And all the demons begged Him, saying, "Send us into the swine, that we may enter into them."

And immediately Jesus gave them leave. And the unclean spirits went out and entered into the swine (they were around two thousand), and the herd ran violently down a steep place into the sea and were choked in the sea. *Mark 5:1–13*

SEE PARALLEL ACCOUNTS AT MATTHEW 8:28–34 AND LUKE 8:27–37

## 84. A WITNESS PLANTED AMONG THE GENTILES

And those who fed the swine fled and told it in the city and in the country. And they went out to see what it was that had happened. And they came to Jesus and saw him who was possessed with the demon and had the legion sitting and clothed and in his right mind. And they were afraid.

And those who saw it told them how it happened to him who was possessed with the demon, and also concerning the swine. And they began to ask Him to depart out of their region.

And when He came into the ship, he who had been possessed with the demon

Jesus' encounter with this out-of-control man (see section 83) is the most dramatic example of His ability to cast demons out of people. Demonic possession could cause physical problems such as blindness (Matthew 12:22). This suggests that the condition was more than a severe case of mental illness. People with this affliction are also described as having an "unclean spirit." Jesus healed several people with this disability (see sections 35, 89, 103, and 113).

asked Him that he might be with Him. However, Jesus did not permit him but said to him, "Go home to your friends and tell them what great things the Lord has done for you, and how He has had compassion on you."

And he departed and began to proclaim in Decapolis what great things Jesus had done for him. And all men marveled. *Mark 5:14–20*

SEE PARALLEL ACCOUNT AT LUKE 8:38–39

## 85. JAIRUS BEGS JESUS TO HEAL HIS DAUGHTER

And when Jesus had crossed over again by ship to the other side, many people gathered to Him, and He was near the sea.

And behold, one of the rulers of the synagogue, Jairus by name, came. And when he saw Him, he fell at His feet and begged Him greatly, saying, "My little daughter lies at the point of death. I ask You, come and lay Your hands on her, that she may be healed and she shall live."

And Jesus went with him, and many people followed Him and thronged Him. *Mark 5:21–24*

SEE PARALLEL ACCOUNTS AT MATTHEW 9:18–19 AND LUKE 8:40–42

## 86. A WOMAN WITH A HEMORRHAGE HEALED

And a certain woman who had a discharge of blood for twelve years, and had suffered many things of many physicians, and had spent all that she had and was no better but rather grew worse, when she had heard of Jesus, came in the crowd behind Him and touched His garment.

For she said, "If I may but touch His clothes, I shall be healed." And immediately the flow of her blood was dried up, and she felt in her body that she was healed of that plague.

And Jesus, knowing in Himself that power had gone out of Him, immediately turned Himself around in the crowd and said, "Who touched My clothes?"

And His disciples said to Him, "You see the multitude thronging You, and yet

You say, 'Who touched Me?'"

And He looked around to see who had done this thing. But the woman, fearing and trembling, knowing what had been done in her, came and fell down before Him and told Him all the truth.

And He said to her, "Daughter, your faith has made you well. Go in peace, and be healed of your plague." *Mark 5:25–34*

SEE PARALLEL ACCOUNTS AT MATTHEW 9:20–22 AND LUKE 8:43–48

Despite the jostling of the crowd, Jesus could tell when a
particular woman touched His garment in hopes of a healing.

## 87. JAIRUS'S DAUGHTER RESTORED TO LIFE

While He [Jesus] was still speaking [to the woman He had healed], some people came from the ruler of the synagogue's [Jairus's] house who said, "Your daughter is dead. Why do you trouble the Master any further?"

As soon as Jesus heard the word that was spoken, He said to the ruler of the synagogue, "Do not be afraid; only believe." And He allowed no man to follow Him except Peter and James and John the brother of James.

And He came to the house of the ruler of the synagogue and saw the tumult and those who wept and wailed greatly. And when He came in, He said to them, "Why do you make this trouble and weep? The child is not dead but is asleep."

And they laughed Him to scorn. But when He had put them all out, He took the father and the mother of the child, and those who were with Him, and entered

Jesus raises Jairus's daughter from the dead.

in where the child was lying. And He took the child by the hand and said to her, "Talitha cumi," which, being interpreted, is, "Little girl, I say to you, arise."

And immediately the child arose and walked, for she was twelve years of age. And they were astonished with a great astonishment. And He charged them strictly that no man should know it and commanded that something should be given to her to eat. *Mark 5:35–43*

See parallel accounts at Matthew 9:23–26 and Luke 8:49–56

## 88. TWO BLIND MEN HEALED

And when Jesus departed from there, two blind men followed Him, crying and saying, "Son of David, have mercy on us." And when He had come into the house, the blind men came to Him. And Jesus said to them, "Do you believe that I am able to do this?"

### A "DON'T TELL" POLICY

Jesus' instructions to these two blind men not to tell anyone about this miracle (see section 88) is often referred to as the "Messianic Secret." He knew that the Jewish people were expecting the Messiah to be a powerful military deliverer. So He downplayed His miraculous works to keep from stirring up their false hopes (see also sections 37, 107, and 108). He was determined to avoid distractions and fulfill His mission as a spiritual Savior.

They said to Him, "Yes, Lord."

Then He touched their eyes, saying, "According to your faith let it be done to you." And their eyes were opened. And Jesus strictly charged them, saying, "See that no man knows it." But they, when they had departed, spread the news about Him in all that country. *Matthew 9:27–31*

The Gospel writer Matthew reports that Jesus went "healing all manner of sickness and all manner of disease among the people" (4:23).

## 89. A DEAF MAN POSSESSED BY DEMONS HEALED

As they [the two healed blind men] went out, behold, they [people in the crowd] brought to Him [Jesus] a mute man possessed with a demon. And when the demon was cast out, the mute man spoke. And the multitudes marveled, saying, "This has never been seen in Israel."

But the Pharisees said, "He casts out demons through the prince of the demons." *Matthew 9:32–34*

## 90. JESUS REJECTED AGAIN IN HIS HOMETOWN

And He [Jesus] went out from there and came into His own country, and His disciples followed Him. And when the Sabbath day came, He began to teach in the synagogue.

And many who heard Him were astonished, saying, "From where did this man get these things? And what wisdom is this that is given to Him, that even such mighty works are worked by His hands? Is not this the carpenter, the son of Mary, the brother of James and Joseph, and of Judas and Simon? And are His sisters not here with us?" And they took offense at Him.

But Jesus said to them, "A prophet is not without honor but in his own country and among his own relatives and in his own house." And He could do no mighty work there, except that He laid His hands on a few sick folk and healed them. And He marveled because of their unbelief. *Mark 6:1–6*

SEE PARALLEL ACCOUNT AT MATTHEW 13:53–58

At times, Jesus' disciples followed Him from place to place. At other times, He sent them out to teach and heal.

## 91. A SPECIAL MISSION FOR THE TWELVE

And Jesus went around to all the cities and villages, teaching in their synagogues, and preaching the gospel of the kingdom, and healing every sickness and every disease among the people. But when He saw the multitudes, He was moved with compassion for them, because they were without hope and were scattered, like sheep having no shepherd.

Then He said to His disciples, "The harvest truly is plenteous, but the laborers are few. Therefore pray to the Lord of the harvest, that He will send forth laborers into His harvest."

And when He had called His twelve disciples to Him, He gave them power against unclean spirits, to cast them out, and to heal all kinds of sickness and all kinds of disease.

Now the names of the twelve apostles are these: the first, Simon, who is called Peter, and Andrew his brother; James the son of Zebedee, and John his brother; Philip, and Bartholomew; Thomas, and Matthew the tax collector; James the son of Alphaeus, and Lebbaeus, whose surname was Thaddaeus; Simon the Canaanite and Judas Iscariot, who also betrayed Him.

Jesus sent forth these twelve and commanded them, saying, "Do not go into the way of the Gentiles, and do not enter into any city of the Samaritans. But go rather to the lost sheep of the house of Israel. And as you go, preach, saying, 'The kingdom of heaven is at hand.'

"Heal the sick, cleanse the lepers, raise the dead, cast out demons. Freely you have received; freely give." *Matthew 9:35–10:8*

SEE PARALLEL ACCOUNTS AT MARK 6:7 AND LUKE 9:1–2

## 92. GUIDELINES FOR THIS MISSION

[Jesus told His disciples whom He sent out]: "Provide neither gold nor silver nor brass in your purses, nor satchel for your journey, nor two coats, nor shoes, nor staffs. For the workman is worthy of his food.

"And whatever city or town you enter into, inquire who is worthy in it, and abide there till you go from there. And when you come into a house, greet it. And if the house is worthy, let your peace come on it. But if it is not worthy, let your peace return to you.

"And whoever does not receive you or hear your words, when you depart out of that house or city, shake the dust off your feet. Truly I say to you, it shall be more tolerable for the land of Sodom and Gomorrah on the day of judgment than for that city.

### "Wise as Serpents. . .Harmless as Doves"

"Behold, I send you forth as sheep in the midst of wolves. Therefore be wise as serpents and harmless as doves. But beware of men, for they will deliver you up to the councils, and they will scourge you in their synagogues. And you shall be brought before governors and kings for My sake, for a testimony against them and the Gentiles.

"But when they deliver you up, do not worry how or what you shall speak. For in that same hour it shall be given you what you shall speak. For it is not you who speak, but the Spirit of your Father who speaks in you.

"And the brother shall deliver up the brother to death, and the father the child. And the children shall rise up against their parents and cause them to be put to death. And you shall be hated by all men for My name's sake. But he who endures to the end shall be saved. But when they persecute you in this city, flee to another. For truly I say to you, you shall not have gone through the cities of Israel before the Son of Man comes.

"The disciple is not above his master, nor the servant above his lord. It is enough for the disciple that he be like his master, and the servant like his lord. If they have called the master of the house Beelzebub, how much more shall they call those of his household?

"Therefore do not fear them. For there is nothing covered that shall not be revealed, and hidden that shall not be known. What I tell you in darkness, speak in the light. And what you hear in the ear, preach on the housetops. And do not fear those who kill the body but are not able to kill the soul. But rather fear Him who is able to destroy both soul and body in hell.

## "You Are of More Value Than Many Sparrows"

"Aren't two sparrows sold for a farthing? And not one of them shall fall on the ground without your Father. But the very hairs of your head are all numbered. Therefore do not fear; you are of more value than many sparrows.

"Therefore whoever confesses Me before men, I will also confess him before My Father who is in heaven. But whoever denies Me before men, I will also deny him before My Father who is in heaven.

## DISCIPLES IN TRAINING

The mission on which Jesus sent His disciples (sections 91 and 92) was a valuable training exercise for the Twelve. He wanted to see how they could apply what they had learned during His ministry with them in Galilee.

Jesus told the disciples to travel light and depend on those to whom they witnessed for their meals and lodging. This is similar to the instructions He gave to seventy of His followers at a later time when He sent them on a similar venture (see section 131). These witnesses were not to waste time, and they should focus on those who were open and receptive to their message.

The daughter of Herodias
receives the head of John
the Baptist on a platter.

"Do not think that I have come to send peace on earth. I came to send not peace but a sword. For I have come to set a man at variance against his father, and the daughter against her mother, and the daughter-in-law against her mother-in-law. And a man's enemies shall be those of his own household.

"He who loves father or mother more than Me is not worthy of Me. And he who loves son or daughter more than Me is not worthy of Me. And he who does not take his cross and follow after Me is not worthy of Me. He who finds his life shall lose it, and he who loses his life for My sake shall find it." *Matthew 10:9–39*

SEE PARALLEL ACCOUNTS AT MARK 6:8–13 AND LUKE 9:3–6

## 93. JOHN THE BAPTIST EXECUTED BY HEROD

For Herod himself had sent forth and taken hold of John and bound him in prison for the sake of Herodias, his brother Philip's wife, for he had married her. For John had said to Herod, "It is not lawful for you to have your brother's wife."

Therefore Herodias had a grudge against him and wanted to kill him, but she could not, for Herod feared John, knowing that he was a just and holy man, and he protected him. And when he heard him, he did many things, and heard him gladly.

And an opportune day came when Herod on his birthday made a supper for his lords, high captains, and chief nobles of Galilee. And when the daughter of Herodias came in and danced, and pleased Herod and those who sat with him, the king said to the girl, "Ask whatever you want from me, and I will give it to you." And he swore to her, "Whatever you shall ask of me, I will give it to you, up to half of my kingdom."

And she went out and said to her mother, "What shall I ask?"

And she said, "The head of John the Baptist."

And she came in immediately in a hurry to the king and asked, saying, "I want you give me at once the head of John the Baptist on a platter."

And the king was exceedingly sorry, yet he would not reject her for his oath's sake and for the sakes of those who sat with him. And immediately the king sent an executioner and commanded his head to be brought. And he went and beheaded him in the prison and brought his head on a platter and gave it to the girl. And the girl gave it to her mother.

### NO GREATER PROPHET

Before John the Baptist was executed, Jesus had said of him, "Among those who are born of women there is not a greater prophet than John the Baptist" (Luke 7:28). The death of His forerunner seemed to be the catalyst that turned Jesus' ministry in a different direction. He began to focus on getting His disciples ready for the future. Perhaps He realized with new urgency that His ministry would be brief like John's and would end with His own violent death.

And when his [John's] disciples heard of it, they came and took his body and laid it in a tomb. *Mark 6:17–29*

SEE PARALLEL ACCOUNT AT MATTHEW 14:3–12

## 94. HEROD'S CURIOSITY ABOUT JESUS

And King Herod heard of Him [Jesus], for His name had spread abroad. And he said, "John the Baptist has risen from the dead, and therefore mighty works show forth themselves in Him."

Others said, "It is Elijah." And others said, "It is a prophet, or similar to one of the prophets." But when Herod heard of it, he said, "It is John, whom I beheaded. He has risen from the dead." *Mark 6:14–16*

SEE PARALLEL ACCOUNT AT LUKE 9:7–9

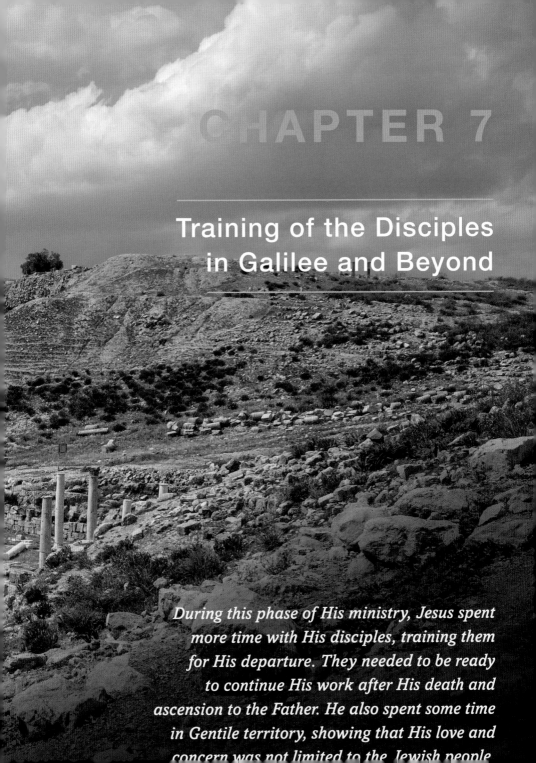

# CHAPTER 7

## Training of the Disciples in Galilee and Beyond

*During this phase of His ministry, Jesus spent more time with His disciples, training them for His departure. They needed to be ready to continue His work after His death and ascension to the Father. He also spent some time in Gentile territory, showing that His love and concern was not limited to the Jewish people.*

## 95. A TIME OF REST WITH THE TWELVE

And the apostles gathered themselves together to Jesus and told Him all things, both what they had done and what they had taught.

And He said to them, "Come by yourselves to a deserted place and rest a while." For there were many coming and going, and they had no leisure even to eat. And they departed privately by ship into a deserted place.

And the people saw them departing, and many knew Him and ran on foot out from all the cities, and went ahead of them and came together to Him. *Mark 6:30–33*

## 96. A MEAGER MEAL FEEDS A CROWD

And Jesus went up on a mountain, and there He sat with His disciples. And the Passover, a feast of the Jews, was near. Then when Jesus lifted up His eyes and saw a great company coming to Him, He said to Philip, "Where shall we buy bread, that these may eat?" And He said this to test him, for He Himself knew what He would do.

Andrew introduces a boy with a lunch to Jesus.

Philip answered him, "Two hundred denarii worth of bread is not sufficient for them, that every one of them may take a little."

## "What Are They Among So Many?"

One of His disciples, Andrew, Simon Peter's brother, said to Him, "There is a lad here who has five barley loaves and two small fish, but what are they among so many?"

And Jesus said, "Make the men sit down." Now there was much grass in the place. So the men sat down, in number about five thousand. And Jesus took the loaves, and when He had given thanks, He distributed to the disciples, and the disciples to those who were sitting down, and likewise of the fishes, as much as they wanted.

When they were filled, He said to His disciples, "Gather up the fragments that remain, that nothing is lost." Therefore they gathered them together and filled twelve baskets with the fragments of the five barley loaves that remained, left over by those who had eaten.

Then those men, when they had seen the miracle that Jesus did, said, "This is truly that Prophet who should come into the world." Therefore when Jesus perceived that they would come and take Him by force to make Him a king, He departed again to a mountain by Himself alone. *John 6:3–15*

### TWO FEEDING MIRACLES

The feeding of the five thousand (see section 96) is the only miracle of Jesus that appears in all four Gospels (Matthew 14:13–23; Mark 6:30–44; Luke 9:10–17). It occurred when people followed Him and the disciples to an isolated place near the Sea of Galilee.

Later, Jesus also multiplied a few pieces of bread and fish to feed a group of people in a Gentile region known as the Decapolis (see section 105). This miracle emphasized His acceptance of all people, regardless of their racial heritage.

## 97. A WALK ON THE WATER

And immediately Jesus compelled His disciples to get into a ship and to go before Him to the other side, while He sent the multitudes away. And when He had sent the multitudes away, He went up by Himself on a mountain to pray. And when the evening came, He was there alone. But the ship was now in the midst of the sea, tossed with waves, for the wind was contrary.

And in the fourth watch of the night Jesus went to them, walking on the sea. And when the disciples saw Him walking on the sea, they were troubled, saying, "It is a spirit." And they cried out in fear.

But immediately Jesus spoke to them, saying, "Be of good cheer. It is I; do not be afraid."

And Peter answered Him and said, "Lord, if it is You, bid me to come to You on the water."

Jesus rescues Peter from the churning waves of the Sea of Galilee.

And He said, "Come."

And when Peter came down out of the ship, he walked on the water to go to Jesus. But when he saw the wind was boisterous, he was afraid. And beginning to sink, he cried, saying, "Lord, save me!"

And immediately Jesus stretched out His hand and caught him, and said to him, "O you of little faith, why did you doubt?" And when they came into the ship, the wind ceased.

Then those who were in the ship came and worshipped Him, saying, "Truly You are the Son of God." *Matthew 14:22–33*

SEE PARALLEL ACCOUNTS AT MARK 6:45–51 AND JOHN 6:16–21

## 98. STRENGTH FROM THE BREAD OF LIFE

The day following, when the people who stood on the other side of the sea saw that there was no other boat there, except the one that His [Jesus'] disciples had entered, and that Jesus did not go with His disciples into the boat, but that His disciples had gone away alone (although there were other boats from Tiberias near the place where they ate bread after the Lord had given thanks), therefore when the people saw that Jesus was not there, nor His disciples, they also got into ships and came to Capernaum, seeking Jesus.

And when they had found Him on the other side of the sea, they said to Him, "Rabbi, when did You come here?"

### JESUS AS THE GREAT "I AM"

Jesus' claim to be the bread of life (see section 98) is one of several "I am" statements He made in the Gospels. The others are:
- "I am the light of the world" (section 123)
- "Before Abraham was, I am" (section 125)
- "I am the door" (section 129)
- "I am the good shepherd" (section 130)
- "I am the resurrection and the life" (section 156)
- "I am the way, the truth, and the life" (section 205)
- "I am the true vine" (section 207)

### "Labor Not for the Food that Perishes"

Jesus answered them and said, "Truly, truly, I say to you, you seek Me, not because you saw the miracles, but because you ate of the loaves and were filled. Labor not for the food that perishes but for that food that endures to everlasting life, which the Son of Man shall give to you, for God the Father has sealed Him."

Then they said to Him, "What shall we do, that we might work the works of God?"

Jesus answered and said to them, "This is the work of God, that you believe in Him whom He has sent."

Therefore they said to Him, "What sign will You show then, that we may see and believe You? What work do you do? Our fathers ate manna in the desert. As it is written, 'He gave them bread from heaven to eat.'"

In His "I Am" statements, Jesus affirmed His unique status as the Son of God.

### "True Bread from Heaven"

Then Jesus said to them, "Truly, truly, I say to you, Moses did not give you that bread from heaven, but My Father gives you the true bread from heaven. For the bread of God is He who comes down from heaven and gives life to the world."

Then they said to Him, "Lord, always give us this bread."

And Jesus said to them, "I am the bread of life. He who comes to Me shall never hunger, and he who believes in Me shall never thirst. But I said to you that you also have seen Me and do not believe. All that the Father gives Me shall come to Me, and the one who comes to Me I will in no way cast out." *John 6:22–37*

## 99. RELIGIOUS LEADERS DISPUTE JESUS' CLAIM

The Jews then murmured at Him [Jesus] because He said, "I am the bread that came down from heaven." And they said, "Is not this Jesus, the son of Joseph, whose father and mother we know? How is it then that He says, 'I came down from heaven'?"

Therefore Jesus answered and said to them, "Do not murmur among yourselves. No man can come to Me unless the Father who has sent Me draws him. And I will raise him up on the last day. It is written in the prophets, 'And they shall all be taught by God.' Therefore every man who has heard and has learned from the Father comes to Me. Not that any man has seen the Father, except He who is from God. He has seen the Father.

### "He Who Believes in Me Has Everlasting Life"

"Truly, truly, I say to you, he who believes in Me has everlasting life. I am that bread of life. Your fathers ate manna in the wilderness and are dead. This is the bread that comes down from heaven, that a man may eat of it and not die. I am the living bread that came down from heaven. If any man eats of this bread, he shall live forever. And the bread that I will give is My flesh, which I will give for the life of the world."

Therefore the Jews argued among themselves, saying, "How can this man give us His flesh to eat?"

Then Jesus said to them, "Truly, truly, I say to you, unless you eat the flesh of the Son of Man and drink His blood, you have no life in you. Whoever eats My flesh and drinks My blood has eternal life, and I will raise him up on the last day. For My flesh is food indeed, and My blood is drink indeed." *John 6:41–55*

## 100. TRADITIONS OF THE PHARISEES IGNORED

Then the Pharisees and some of the scribes who came from Jerusalem came together to Him [Jesus]. And when they saw some of His disciples eating bread with defiled—that is to say, with unwashed—hands, they found fault.

Moses with the original Ten Commandments. Jesus criticized the Pharisees for making their additions to these divine commands more important than the law itself.

For the Pharisees and all the Jews do not eat unless they wash their hands often, holding the tradition of the elders. And when they come from the market, they do not eat unless they wash. And there are many other things that they have received and hold to, such as the washing of cups and pots, brass vessels, and tables.

Then the Pharisees and scribes asked Him, "Why do Your disciples not walk according to the tradition of the elders but eat bread with unwashed hands?" *Mark 7:1–5*

SEE PARALLEL ACCOUNT AT MATTHEW 15:1–6

## 101. DIVINE COMMANDS OR HUMAN TRADITIONS?

He [Jesus] answered and said to them [Pharisees and scribes], "Isaiah prophesied well of you hypocrites, as it is written: 'This people honors Me with their lips, but their heart is far from Me. However they worship Me in vain, teaching the commandments of men for doctrines.'

"For laying aside the commandment of God, you hold to the tradition of men, such as the washing of pots and cups, and you do many other similar things."

And He said to them, "Full well you reject the commandment of God, that you may keep your own tradition. For Moses said, 'Honor your father and your mother,' and, 'Whoever curses father or mother, let him be put to death.'

"But you say, 'If a man says to his father or mother, "It is Corban—that is to say, a gift—by whatever you might have profited from me," he shall be free.' And you no longer allow him to do anything for his father or his mother, making the word of God of no effect through your tradition that you have delivered. And you do many similar things." *Mark 7:6–13*

SEE PARALLEL ACCOUNT AT MATTHEW 15:7–11

## 102. INNER PURITY OR EXTERNAL RITUALS?

Then His [Jesus'] disciples came and said to Him, "Do you know that the Pharisees were offended after they heard this saying?"

But He answered and said, "Every plant that My heavenly Father has not planted shall be rooted up. Leave them alone. They are blind leaders of the blind. And if the blind leads the blind, both shall fall into the ditch."

Then Peter answered and said to Him, "Declare this parable to us."

And Jesus said, "Are you also still without understanding? Do you not yet understand that whatever enters in at the mouth goes into the belly and is cast out into the latrine? But those things that proceed out of the mouth come forth from the heart, and they defile the man.

"For out of the heart proceed evil thoughts, murders, adulteries, fornications, thefts, false witness, blasphemies. These are the things that defile a man, but to eat with unwashed hands does not defile a man." *Matthew 15:12–20*

Then Jesus went from there and departed into the region of Tyre and Sidon. And behold, a woman of Canaan came out of the same region and cried to Him, saying, "Have mercy on me, O Lord, Son of David. My daughter is grievously vexed with a demon."

But He did not answer her a word. And His disciples came and implored Him, saying, "Send her away, for she cries after us."

But He answered and said, "I was sent only to the lost sheep of the house of Israel."

Then she came and worshipped Him, saying, "Lord, help me."

But He answered and said, "It is not proper to take the children's bread and to cast it to dogs."

And she said, "True, Lord, yet the dogs eat of the crumbs that fall from their masters' table."

Jesus' healing of a Gentile girl affirms that He was the Good Shepherd.

Then Jesus answered and said to her, "O woman, great is your faith. May it be to you just as you desire." And her daughter was healed from that very hour. *Matthew 15:21–28*

SEE PARALLEL ACCOUNT AT MARK 7:24–30

## 104. A DEAF MAN HEALED IN GENTILE TERRITORY

And again, departing from the region of Tyre and Sidon, He [Jesus] came to the Sea of Galilee, through the midst of the region of Decapolis.

And they brought to Him one who was deaf and had an impediment in his speech, and they begged Him to put His hand on him. And He took him aside from the multitude and put His fingers into his ears, and He spit and touched his tongue. And looking up to heaven, He sighed and said to him, "Ephphatha" (that is, "Be opened"). And immediately his ears were opened, and the string of his tongue was released, and he spoke plainly.

And He charged them that they should tell no man, but the more He charged them, the more they proclaimed it a great deal. And they were astonished beyond measure, saying, "He has done all things well. He makes both the deaf to hear and the mute to speak." *Mark 7:31–37*

## 105. A HUNGRY CROWD OF GENTILES FED

And great multitudes came to Him [Jesus], having with them those who were lame, blind, mute, maimed, and many others, and laid them down at Jesus' feet, and He healed them, to such a degree that the multitude wondered when they saw the mute speaking, the maimed made whole, the lame walking, and the blind seeing. And they glorified the God of Israel.

Then Jesus called His disciples to Him and said, "I have compassion on the multitude, because they have now continued with Me three days and have nothing to eat. And I will not send them away fasting, lest they faint on the way."

And His disciples said to Him, "From where should we get so much bread in the wilderness as to feed so great a multitude?"

And Jesus said to them, "How many loaves do you have?"

And they said, "Seven, and a few little fish."

And He commanded the multitude to sit down on the ground. And He took the seven loaves and the fish and gave thanks, and broke them and gave them to His disciples. And the disciples gave them to the multitude.

And they all ate and were filled, and they took up seven baskets full of the broken food that was left. And those who ate were four thousand men, besides women and children. *Matthew 15:30–38*

SEE PARALLEL ACCOUNT AT MARK 8:1–9

## 106. BEWARE OF THE PHARISEES AND SADDUCEES

And when His disciples had come to the other side, they had forgotten to take bread. Then Jesus said to them, "Be careful and beware of the leaven of the Pharisees and of the Sadducees."

And they reasoned among themselves, saying, "It is because we have taken no bread."

When Jesus perceived this, He said to them, "O you of little faith, why do you reason among yourselves because you have brought no bread? Do you not yet understand or remember the five loaves of the five thousand and how many baskets you took up? Nor the seven loaves of the four thousand and how many baskets you took up?

"How is it that you do not understand that I did not speak to you concerning bread, but that you should beware of the leaven of the Pharisees and of the Sadducees?"

Then they understood that He told them to beware not of the leaven of bread but of the doctrine of the Pharisees and of the Sadducees. *Matthew 16:5–12*

SEE PARALLEL ACCOUNT AT MARK 8:13–21

### DANGEROUS DOCTRINES

Jesus had no patience with the teachings of the Pharisees and Sadducees (see section 106). The legalistic Pharisees considered their traditions more important than the clear teachings of scripture. And the Sadducees were known for their denial of the reality of the afterlife. Jesus condemned both groups for their false doctrines several times during His ministry (see sections 48, 101, 136, 187, and 188).

## 107. A BLIND MAN HEALED AT BETHSAIDA

And He [Jesus] came to Bethsaida. And they brought a blind man to Him and begged Him to touch him. And He took the blind man by the hand and led him out of the town. And when He had spit on his eyes and put His hands on him, He asked him if he saw anything.

And he looked up and said, "I see men as trees, walking."

After that He put His hands on his eyes again and made him look up. And he was restored and saw every man clearly. And He sent him away to his house, saying, "Do not go into the town or tell it to anyone in the town." *Mark 8:22–26*

Site of the ancient city of Caesarea Philippi, where Peter declared that Jesus was the promised Messiah.

## 108. PETER'S GREAT CONFESSION: "YOU ARE THE CHRIST"

When Jesus came into the region of Caesarea Philippi, He asked His disciples, saying, "Who do men say that I, the Son of Man, am?"

And they said, "Some say that You are John the Baptist, some Elijah, and others Jeremiah or one of the prophets."

He said to them, "But who do you say that I am?"

And Simon Peter answered and said, "You are the Christ, the Son of the living God."

And Jesus answered and said to him, "Blessed are you, Simon Bar-Jonah, for flesh and blood has not revealed it to you, but My Father who is in heaven. And I also say to you that you are Peter, and on this rock I will build My church, and the gates of hell shall not prevail against it. And I will give to you the keys of the kingdom of heaven, and whatever you bind on earth shall be bound in heaven, and whatever you loose on earth shall be loosed in heaven."

Then He charged His disciples that they should tell no man that He was Jesus the Christ. *Matthew 16:13–20*

SEE PARALLEL ACCOUNTS AT MARK 8:27–30 AND LUKE 9:18–20

123

## 109. JESUS PREDICTS HIS DEATH

From that time forth Jesus began to show to His disciples that He must go to Jerusalem, and suffer many things from the elders and chief priests and scribes, and be killed, and be raised again the third day.

Then Peter took Him and began to rebuke Him, saying, "Far be it from You, Lord. This shall not happen to You."

But He turned and said to Peter, "Get behind Me, Satan. You are a stumbling block to Me, for you appreciate the things that are of men, but not those that are of God." *Matthew 16:21–23*

SEE PARALLEL ACCOUNTS AT MARK 8:31–33 AND LUKE 9:21–22

## 110. A CROSS FOR JESUS' FOLLOWERS

And when He [Jesus] had called the people to Himself, with His disciples also, He said to them, "Whoever wants to come after Me, let Him deny himself, and take up his cross, and follow Me. For whoever wants to save his life shall lose it, but whoever shall lose his life for My sake and the gospel's, the same shall save it.

"For what shall it profit a man if he gains the whole world and loses his own soul? Or what shall a man give in exchange for his soul?" *Mark 8:34–37*

SEE PARALLEL ACCOUNTS AT LUKE 9:23–25

## 111. ASSURANCE OF JESUS' RETURN

[Jesus said]: "Therefore whoever shall be ashamed of Me and of My words in this adulterous and sinful generation, the Son of Man shall also be ashamed of him when He comes in the glory of His Father with the holy angels."

And He said to them, "Truly I say to you that there are some of those who stand here who shall not taste of death till they have seen the kingdom of God come with power." *Mark 8:38–9:1*

SEE PARALLEL ACCOUNTS AT MATTHEW 16:27–28 AND LUKE 9:26–27

Jesus carries His cross—
a symbol of the commitment to
discipleship required of all believers.

Jesus talks with Moses and Elijah as Peter, James, and John marvel at the change in His appearance.

## 112. A GLORIOUS TRANSFIGURATION

And it came to pass, about eight days after these sayings, He [Jesus] took Peter and John and James and went up on a mountain to pray. And as He prayed, the appearance of His face was altered, and His clothing was white and glistening. And behold, two men talked with Him, who were Moses and Elijah, who appeared in glory and spoke of His death that He was about to accomplish in Jerusalem.

But Peter and those who were with him were heavy with sleep, and when they were awake, they saw His glory and the two men who stood with Him. And it came to pass, as they departed from Him, Peter said to Jesus, "Master, it is good for us to be here. And let us make three tabernacles: one for You, and one for Moses, and one for Elijah"—not knowing what he said.

### AN ENCOURAGING FATHER

This divine declaration at Jesus' Transfiguration (section 112) is one of three separate times when God the Father spoke in an audible voice to encourage His Son. God commended Jesus' actions at His baptism when he launched His public ministry (section 22). He also assured His Son as He faced the cross that His death would bring glory to the Father (section 177).

While he was saying this, a cloud came and overshadowed them, and they feared as they entered into the cloud. And a voice came out of the cloud, saying, "This is My beloved Son. Hear Him." And when the voice was past, Jesus was found alone. And they kept quiet and told no one in those days any of the things that they had seen. *Luke 9:28–36*

SEE PARALLEL ACCOUNTS AT MATTHEW 17:1–8 AND MARK 9:2–8

## 113. A STUBBORN DEMON CAST OUT OF A BOY

And when they [Jesus and His disciples] had come to the multitude, there came to Him a certain man, kneeling down to Him and saying, "Lord, have mercy on my son, for he is insane and greatly vexed. For often he falls into the fire and often into the water. And I brought him to Your disciples, and they could not cure him."

Then Jesus answered and said, "O faithless and perverse generation, how long shall I be with you? How long shall I bear with you? Bring him here to Me." And Jesus rebuked the demon, and he departed out of him. And the child was cured from that very hour.

Then the disciples came to Jesus by themselves and said, "Why could we not cast him out?"

And Jesus said to them, "Because of your unbelief. For truly, I say to you, if you have faith as a grain of mustard seed, you shall say to this mountain, 'Move from here to there,' and it shall move, and nothing shall be impossible for you. Although this kind does not go out but by prayer and fasting." *Matthew 17:14–21*

SEE PARALLEL ACCOUNTS AT MARK 9:14–29 AND LUKE 9:37–42

## 114. A MIRACULOUS COIN FOR THE TEMPLE TAX

And when they [Jesus and His disciples] had come to Capernaum, those who received tribute money came to Peter and said, "Does your Master not pay tribute?"

He said, "Yes."

And when he had come into the house, Jesus said to him first, "What do you think, Simon? From whom do the kings of the earth take custom or tribute? From their own children or from strangers?"

Peter said to Him, "From strangers."

Jesus said to him, "Then the children are free. However, lest we should offend them, go to the sea and cast a hook, and take up the first fish that comes up. And when you have opened its mouth, you shall find a piece of money. Take that and give it to them for Me and you." *Matthew 17:24–27*

This Roman coin may be like the one that Jesus produced to pay the temple tax required of all Jewish males.

## 115. DRAMATIC ACTION FOR A SERIOUS PROBLEM

[Jesus said]: "Whoever causes one of these little ones who believes in Me to stumble, it would be better for him if a millstone were hung around his neck and he were cast into the sea.

"And if your hand causes you to stumble, cut it off. It is better for you to enter into life maimed than, having two hands, to go into hell, into the fire that shall never be quenched, where 'their worm does not die and the fire is not quenched.'

"And if your foot causes you to stumble, cut it off! It is better for you to enter lame into life than, having two feet, to be cast into hell, into the fire that never shall be quenched, where 'their worm does not die and the fire is not quenched.'

"And if your eye offends you, pluck it out! It is better for you to enter into the kingdom of God with one eye than, having two eyes, to be cast into hellfire, where 'their worm does not die and the fire is not quenched.'

"For everyone shall be salted with fire, and every sacrifice shall be salted with salt. Salt is good, but if the salt has lost its saltiness, with what will you season it? Have salt in yourselves, and have peace with one another." *Mark 9:42–50*

SEE PARALLEL ACCOUNT AT MATTHEW 18:6–10

## WHAT TO DO ABOUT SIN

Jesus' statement about cutting off an offensive hand or foot (see section 115) is a good example of an expression known as hyperbole, or deliberate overstatement to drive home a point. This was His way of declaring that sin is a serious problem and must be dealt with in forceful fashion.

Another example of this technique is Jesus' charge that the Pharisees—because of their extreme literalism—were guilty of straining at a gnat but gulping down a camel (see section 188).

## 116. A PRESCRIPTION FOR CONFLICT

[Jesus said]: "Moreover, if your brother trespasses against you, go and tell him his fault between you and him alone. If he hears you, you have gained your brother. But if he will not hear you, then take with you one or two more, that in the mouth of two or three witnesses every word may be established.

"And if he neglects to hear them, tell it to the church. But if he neglects to hear the church, let him be to you as a heathen man and a tax collector. Truly I say to you, whatever you bind on earth shall be bound in heaven, and whatever you loose on earth shall be loosed in heaven.

"Again I say to you that if two of you agree on earth concerning anything that they ask, it shall be done for them by My Father who is in heaven. For where two or three are gathered together in My name, there I am in the midst of them." *Matthew 18:15–20*

## 117. PARABLE OF THE UNFORGIVING SERVANT

Then Peter came to Him [Jesus] and said, "Lord, how often shall my brother sin against me and I forgive him? Up to seven times?"

Jesus said to him, "I do not say to you, up to seven times, but up to seventy times seven. Therefore the kingdom of heaven is compared to a certain king who would take account of his servants. And when he had begun to settle the accounts, one was brought to him who owed him ten thousand talents.

"But since he could not pay, his lord commanded him to be sold—and his wife, and children, and all that he had—and payment to be made. Therefore the servant fell down and worshipped him, saying, 'Lord, have patience with me, and I will pay you all.' Then the lord of that servant was moved with compassion and released him and forgave him the debt.

Peter's question about forgiveness led to Jesus' parable of the unforgiving servant.

### "Pay Me What You Owe"

"But the same servant went out and found one of his fellow servants who owed him a hundred pence. And he laid hands on him and took him by the throat, saying, 'Pay me what you owe.' And his fellow servant fell down at his feet and begged him, saying, 'Have patience with me, and I will pay you all.' And he would not, but went and cast him into prison till he should pay the debt.

"So when his fellow servants saw what was done, they were very sorry, and came and told to their lord all that had been done. Then his lord, after he had called him, said to him, 'O you wicked servant. I forgave you all that debt because you asked me. Should you not also have had compassion on your fellow servant, even as I had pity on you?'

"And his lord was angry and delivered him to the tormentors till he should pay all that was due to him. So likewise shall My heavenly Father do also to every one of you if you do not forgive your brother his trespasses from your heart." *Matthew 18:21–35*

## 118. JESUS DEMANDS TOTAL COMMITMENT

And it came to pass that, as they [Jesus and His disciples] went on the road, a certain man said to Him, "Lord, I will follow You wherever You go."

And Jesus said to him, "Foxes have holes and birds of the air have nests, but the Son of Man does not have anywhere to lay His head."

And He said to another, "Follow Me."

But he said, "Lord, allow me first to go and bury my father."

Jesus said to him, "Let the dead bury their dead, but you go and preach the kingdom of God."

And another also said, "Lord, I will follow You, but let me first go bid farewell to those who are living at my house."

And Jesus said to him, "No man who puts his hand to the plow and looks back is fit for the kingdom of God." *Luke 9:57–62*

See parallel account at Matthew 8:19–22

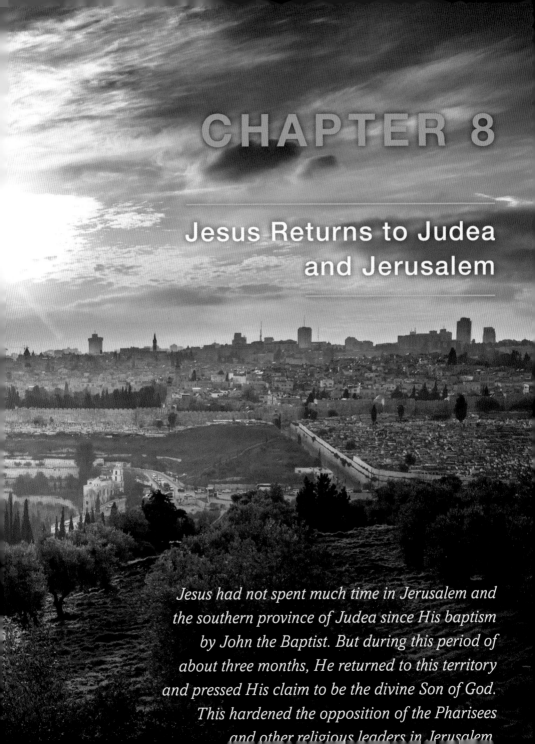

# CHAPTER 8

## Jesus Returns to Judea and Jerusalem

*Jesus had not spent much time in Jerusalem and the southern province of Judea since His baptism by John the Baptist. But during this period of about three months, He returned to this territory and pressed His claim to be the divine Son of God. This hardened the opposition of the Pharisees and other religious leaders in Jerusalem*

## 119. JESUS URGED TO GO TO JERUSALEM

Now the Jews' Feast of Tabernacles was at hand. Therefore His [Jesus'] brothers said to Him, "Depart from here and go into Judea, that Your disciples may also see the works that You are doing. For there is no man who does anything in secret when he himself seeks to be known openly. If You do these things, show Yourself to the world." For His brothers did not believe in Him.

Then Jesus said to them, "My time has not yet come, but your time is always ready. The world cannot hate you, but it hates Me because I testify of it that its works are evil. You go up to this feast. I will not go up yet to this feast, for My time has not yet fully come." When He had said these words to them, He remained in Galilee.

But when His brothers had gone up, then He also went up to the feast, not openly, but as it were in secret. *John 7:2–10*

## 120. A MIXED RECEPTION IN JERUSALEM

Then some of them from Jerusalem said, "Is not this He [Jesus] whom they seek to kill? But, look, He speaks boldly, and they say nothing to Him. Do the rulers indeed know that this is the Christ? However, we know where this man is from, but when Christ comes, no man will know where He is from."

Then Jesus cried out in the temple as He taught, saying, "You both know Me and you know where I am from. And I have not come of Myself, but He who sent me is true, whom you do not know. But I know Him, for I am from Him, and He has sent Me." Then they sought to take Him, but no man laid hands on Him because His hour had not yet come.

And many of the people believed in Him and said, "When Christ comes, will He do more miracles than these that this man has done?"

The Pharisees heard that the people murmured such things concerning Him, and the Pharisees and the chief priests sent officers to take Him. Then Jesus said to them, "I am with you yet a little while, and then I go to Him who sent Me. You shall seek Me and shall not find Me, and where I am you cannot come."

Then the Jews said among themselves, "Where will He go that we shall not find Him? Will He go to the dispersed among the Gentiles, and teach the Gentiles? What manner of saying is this that He said, 'You shall seek Me and shall not find Me, and where I am you cannot come'?" *John 7:25–36*

## 121. JESUS CLAIMS TO BE LIVING WATER

On the last day, that great day of the feast, Jesus stood and cried, saying, "If any man thirsts, let him come to Me and drink. He who believes in Me, as the scripture has said, out of his belly shall flow rivers of living water." (But He spoke this of the Spirit, whom those who believe in Him would receive. For the Holy Spirit was not

Jesus describes Himself as Living Water that quenches spiritual thirst.

yet given, because Jesus was not yet glorified.)

Therefore many of the people, when they heard this saying, said, "Truly this is the Prophet." Others said, "This is the Christ." But some said, "Shall Christ come out of Galilee? Has the scripture not said that Christ comes from the descendants of David and out of the town of Bethlehem, where David was?"

So there was a division among the people because of Him. And some of them would have taken Him, but no man laid hands on Him. *John 7:37–44*

## 122. FORGIVENESS FOR A SINFUL WOMAN

Jesus went to the Mount of Olives. And early in the morning He came again into the temple, and all the people came to Him. And He sat down and taught them. And the scribes and Pharisees brought to Him a woman caught in adultery. And when they had set her in the midst, they said to Him, "Master, this woman was caught in adultery, in the very act. Now Moses, in the Law, commanded us that such should be stoned. But what do You say?"

They said this, tempting Him, that they might have reason to accuse Him. But Jesus stooped down and with His finger wrote on the ground, as though He did

Scribes and Pharisees present a woman accused of adultery to Jesus.

136

not hear them. So when they continued asking Him, He lifted Himself up and said to them, "He who is without sin among you, let him first cast a stone at her." And again He stooped down and wrote on the ground.

And those who heard it, being convicted by their own consciences, went out one by one, beginning at the eldest, even to the last. And Jesus was left alone, and the woman standing in the midst. When Jesus had lifted Himself up and saw none but the woman, He said to her, "Woman, where are those accusers of yours? Has no man condemned you?"

She said, "No man, Lord."

And Jesus said to her, "Neither do I condemn you. Go and sin no more." *John 8:1–11*

## 123. DISPUTE OVER JESUS AS THE LIGHT OF THE WORLD

Then Jesus spoke again to them [the Pharisees], saying, "I am the light of the world. He who follows Me shall not walk in darkness but shall have the light of life."

Therefore the Pharisees said to Him, "You bear witness of Yourself. Your testimony is not true."

Jesus answered and said to them, "Though I bear witness of Myself, yet My witness is true, for I know from where I came and where I go. But you cannot tell from where I come and where I go. You judge according to the flesh; I judge no man.

"And yet if I judge, My judgment is true, for I am not alone, but I and the Father who sent Me. It is also written in your law that the testimony of two men is true. I am one who bears witness of Myself, and the Father who sent Me bears witness of Me."

Then said they to Him, "Where is Your Father?"

Jesus answered, "You know neither Me nor My Father. If you had known Me, You should have known My Father also." Jesus spoke these words in the treasury as He taught in the temple. And no man laid hands on Him, for His hour had not yet come. *John 8:12–20*

## 124. PHARISEES ACCUSED OF COMMITTING SIN

Then Jesus said again to them [Pharisees], "I go My way, and you shall seek Me and shall die in your sins. Where I go you cannot come."

Then the Jews said, "Will He kill Himself, because He said, 'Where I go, you cannot come'?"

And He said to them, "You are from beneath; I am from above. You are of this world; I am not of this world. Therefore I said to you that you shall die in your sins. For if you do not believe that I am He, you shall die in your sins."

Then they said to Him, "Who are You?"

And Jesus said to them, "Even the same that I said to you from the beginning. I have many things to say and to judge of you, but He who sent Me is true. And I speak to the world those things that I have heard from Him." They did not understand that He spoke to them of the Father.

## "He Who Sent Me Is with Me"

Then said Jesus to them, "When you have lifted up the Son of Man, then you shall know that I am He, and that I do nothing of Myself. But as My Father has taught Me, I speak these things. And He who sent Me is with Me. The Father has not left Me alone, for I always do those things that please Him." As He spoke these words, many believed in Him.

Then Jesus said to those Jews who believed in Him, "If you continue in My word, then you are My disciples indeed. And you shall know the truth, and the truth shall make you free."

They answered Him, "We are Abraham's descendants and were never in bondage to any man. How do You say, 'You shall be made free'?"

Jesus answered them, "Truly, truly, I say to you, whoever commits sin is the servant of sin. And the servant does not abide in the house forever, but the Son abides forever. Therefore if the Son shall make you free, you shall be free indeed." *John 8:21–36*

# 125. JESUS' EXISTENCE BEFORE ABRAHAM

[Jesus said]: "I know that you [Pharisees] are Abraham's descendants, but you seek to kill Me because My word has no place in you. I speak what I have seen with My Father, and you do what you have seen with your father."

They answered and said to Him, "Abraham is our father."

Jesus said to them, "If you were Abraham's children, you would do the works of Abraham. But now you seek to kill Me, a man who has told you the truth, which I have heard from God. Abraham did not do this. You do the deeds of your father."

Then they said to Him, "We were not born of fornication. We have one Father, even God."

Jesus said to them, "If God were your Father, you would love Me, for I proceeded forth and came from God. I did not come of Myself, but He sent Me. Why do you not understand My speech? It is because you cannot hear My word.

"You are from your father the devil, and the lusts of your father you will do. He was a murderer from the beginning and abided not in the truth, because there is no truth in him. When he speaks a lie, he speaks of his own, for he is a liar and the father of it.

## "He Who Is of God Hears God's Words"

"And because I tell you the truth, you do not believe Me. Which of you convicts Me of sin? And if I say the truth, why do you not believe Me? He who is of God hears God's words. Therefore you do not hear them, because you are not of God."

Then the Jews answered and said to Him, "Do we not rightly say that You are a Samaritan and have a demon?"

Jesus answered, "I do not have a demon, but I honor my Father, and you dishonor Me. And I do not seek My own glory. There is One who seeks and judges. Truly, truly, I say to you, if a man keeps My saying, he shall never see death."

Jesus minced no words with the Pharisees; He accused them of of being children of Satan.

Then the Jews said to Him, "Now we know that You have a demon. Abraham is dead, and the prophets. And You say, 'If a man keeps My saying, he shall never taste of death.' Are You greater than our father Abraham, who is dead? And the prophets are dead. Who do You make Yourself out to be?"

## "My Father. . .Honors Me"

Jesus answered, "If I honor Myself, My honor is nothing. It is My Father who honors Me, of whom you say that He is your God. Yet you have not known Him, but I know Him. And if I should say, 'I do not know Him,' I shall be a liar like you. But I know Him and keep His saying. Your father Abraham rejoiced to see My day, and he saw it and was glad."

Then the Jews said to Him, "You are not yet fifty years old, and have You seen Abraham?"

Jesus said to them, "Truly, truly, I say to you, before Abraham was, I am." Then they took up stones to cast at Him. But Jesus hid Himself and went out of the temple, going through the midst of them, and so passed by. *John 8:37–59*

Sometimes Jesus would heal with a word. At other times, He used a touch—
even applying His own spit to a blind man's eyes.

## 126. A MAN BORN BLIND HEALED AT JERUSALEM

And as Jesus passed by, He saw a man who was blind from his birth. And His disciples asked Him, saying, "Master, who sinned, this man or his parents, that he was born blind?"

Jesus answered, "Neither this man nor his parents sinned, but that the works of God should be revealed in him. I must work the works of Him who sent Me while it is day. The night comes when no man can work. As long as I am in the world, I am the light of the world."

When He had thus spoken, He spit on the ground and made clay of the saliva. And He anointed the eyes of the blind man with the clay and said to him, "Go, wash in the pool of Siloam" (which is by interpretation, Sent). Therefore he went his way and washed, and came back seeing.

Therefore the neighbors and those who before had seen that he was blind said, "Is this not he who sat and begged?"

Some said, "This is he." Others said, "He is like him."

But he said, "I am he."

Therefore they said to him, "How were your eyes opened?"

He answered and said, "A man who is called Jesus made clay and anointed my eyes and said to me, 'Go to the pool of Siloam and wash.' And I went and washed, and I received sight."

Then said they to him, "Where is He?"

He said, "I do not know." *John 9:1–12*

## 127. PHARISEES DISPUTE THIS MIRACULOUS HEALING

They brought him who formerly was blind to the Pharisees. And it was the Sabbath day when Jesus made the clay and opened his eyes. Then again the Pharisees also asked him how he had received his sight. He said to them, "He put clay on my eyes, and I washed, and I see."

Therefore some of the Pharisees said, "This man is not from God because He does not keep the Sabbath day." Others said, "How can a man who is a sinner do such miracles?" And there was a division among them.

They said to the blind man again, "What do you say about Him, that He has opened your eyes?"

He said, "He is a prophet."

But the Jews did not believe concerning him, that he had been blind and received his sight, until they called the parents of him who had received his sight. And they asked them, saying, "Is this your son, who you say was born blind? How then does he now see?"

## "He Shall Speak for Himself"

His parents answered them and said, "We know that this is our son and that he was born blind, but we do not know by what means he now sees. We do not know who has opened his eyes. He is of age; ask him. He shall speak for himself."

His parents spoke these words because they feared the Jews, for the Jews had already agreed that if any man confessed that He was Christ, he should be put out of the synagogue. Therefore his parents said, "He is of age; ask him."

Then again they [Pharisees] called the man who was blind and said to him, "Give God the praise. We know that this man is a sinner."

## "Although I Was Blind, Now I See"

He answered and said, "Whether He is a sinner or not I do not know. One thing I know: that although I was blind, now I see."

Then they said to him again, "What did He do to you? How did He open your eyes?"

He answered them, "I have told you already, and you did not hear. For what reason would you hear it again? Will you also be His disciples?"

Then they reviled him and said, "You are His disciple, but we are Moses' disciples. We know that God spoke to Moses. As for this fellow, we do not know where He is from."

The man answered and said to them, "Why, here is a marvelous thing, that you do not know where He is from, and yet He has opened my eyes. Now we know that God does not hear sinners, but if any man is a worshipper of God and does His will, He hears him. Since the world began it was not heard that any man opened the eyes of one who was born blind. If this man were not of God, He could do nothing."

They answered and said to him, "You were altogether born in sins, and do you teach us?" And they cast him out. *John 9:13–34*

### THOSE WHO WILL NOT SEE

It's not surprising that the Pharisees would not admit that this blind man had been healed by Jesus (see sections 127 and 128). Their hatred of Jesus led them to oppose everything He did, even this act of mercy. Jesus noted the irony of the situation: The man born blind could now see both physically and spiritually. But the Pharisees continued to grope in the darkness because of their envy and prejudice—the worst kind of blindness.

# 128. THIS BLIND MAN RECEIVES SPIRITUAL SIGHT

Jesus heard that they had cast him [the healed blind man] out, and when He had found him, He said to him, "Do you believe in the Son of God?"

He answered and said, "Who is He, Lord, that I might believe in Him?"

And Jesus said to him, "You have both seen Him and it is He who talks with you."

And he said, "Lord, I believe." And he worshipped Him.

And Jesus said, "For judgment I have come into this world, that those who do not see might see, and that those who see might be made blind."

And some of the Pharisees who were with Him heard these words and said to Him, "Are we blind also?"

Jesus said to them, "If you were blind, you would have no sin. But now you say, 'We see.' Therefore your sin remains." *John 9:35–41*

## 129. RELIGIOUS LEADERS COMPARED TO THIEVES

[Jesus said]: "Truly, truly, I say to you, He who does not enter by the door into the sheepfold, but climbs up some other way, the same is a thief and a robber. But he who enters in by the door is the shepherd of the sheep. To him the doorkeeper opens, and the sheep hear his voice. And he calls his own sheep by name and leads them out.

"And when he brings out his own sheep, he goes before them, and the sheep follow him, for they know his voice. And they will not follow a stranger but will flee from him, for they do not know the voice of strangers."

Jesus spoke this parable to them, but they did not understand what things they were that He spoke to them.

Then Jesus said to them again, "Truly, truly, I say to you, I am the door of the sheep. All who ever came before Me are thieves and robbers, but the sheep did not hear them. I am the door. If any man enters in by Me, he shall be saved and shall go in and out and find pasture.

"The thief does not come except to steal and to kill and to destroy. I have come that they might have life, and that they might have it more abundantly." *John 10:1–10*

## 130. THE GOOD SHEPHERD AND HIS SHEEP

[Jesus said]: "I am the good shepherd. The good shepherd gives His life for the sheep. But he who is a hired hand, and not the shepherd, who does not own the sheep, sees the wolf coming and leaves the sheep and flees. And the wolf catches them and scatters the sheep. The hired hand flees because he is a hired hand and does not care for the sheep.

"I am the good shepherd, and know My sheep, and am known by My own. As the Father knows Me, even so I know the Father, and I lay down My life for the sheep. And I have other sheep that are not of this fold. I must bring them also, and they shall hear My voice. And there shall be one fold and one shepherd.

"Therefore My Father loves Me, because I lay down My life that I might take

Jesus as the Good Shepherd who loves and cares for His sheep.

it again. No man takes it from Me, but I lay it down of Myself. I have power to lay it down, and I have power to take it again. This commandment I have received from My Father."

Therefore there was a division again among the Jews because of these sayings. And many of them said, "He has a demon and is mad. Why do you listen to Him?"

Others said, "These are not the words of Him who has a demon. Can a demon open the eyes of the blind?" *John 10:11–21*

## 131. SEVENTY FOLLOWERS SENT TO TEACH AND HEAL

After these things the Lord appointed seventy others also and sent them two by two before His face into every city and place where He Himself would go. Therefore He said to them, "The harvest is truly great, but the laborers are few. Therefore pray to the Lord of the harvest, that He would send forth laborers into His harvest. Go your way.

"Behold, I send you out as lambs among wolves. Carry neither purse, nor bag, nor shoes, and greet no man on the way. And whatever house you enter into, first say, 'Peace be to this house.' And if the son of peace is there, your peace shall rest on it; if not, it shall return to you.

"And remain in the same house, eating and drinking such things as they give, for the laborer is worthy of his hire. Do not go from house to house. And whatever city you enter into, and they receive you, eat such things as are set before you. And heal the sick who are in it, and say to them, 'The kingdom of God has come near to you.'

"But whatever city you enter into and they do not receive you, go your way out into the streets of the same and say, 'Even the very dust of your city that clings to us we wipe off against you. However, be sure of this, that the kingdom of God has come near to you.' But I say to you that it shall be more tolerable on that day for Sodom than for that city." *Luke 10:1–12*

## 132. REPORT OF A SUCCESSFUL MISSION

And the seventy returned with joy, saying, "Lord, even the demons are subject to us through Your name."

And He said to them, "I saw Satan fall from heaven as lightning. Behold, I give you power to tread on serpents and scorpions, and over all the power of the enemy, and nothing shall hurt you by any means. However, do not rejoice in this, that the spirits are subject to you, but rather rejoice because your names are written in heaven."

In that hour Jesus rejoiced in spirit and said, "I thank You, O Father, Lord of heaven and earth, that You have hidden these things from the wise and prudent and have revealed them to infants. Even so, Father, for so it seemed good in Your

In Jesus' parable, a compassionate Samaritan stops to help a wounded man
while two religious authorities ignore the victim's plight.

sight. All things are delivered to Me by My Father, and no man knows who the
Son is but the Father, and who the Father is but the Son, and he to whom the Son
will reveal Him."

And He turned to His disciples and said privately, "Blessed are the eyes that see
the things that you see. For I tell you that many prophets and kings have desired to
see those things that you see and have not seen them, and to hear those things that
you hear and have not heard them." *Luke 10:17–24*

## 133. PARABLE OF THE GOOD SAMARITAN

And, behold, a certain lawyer stood up and tempted Him [Jesus], saying, "Master,
what shall I do to inherit eternal life?"

He said to him, "What is written in the law? How do you read it?"

And he answered and said, "'You shall love the Lord your God with all your
heart, and with all your soul, and with all your strength, and with all your mind,'
and 'your neighbor as yourself.'"

And He said to him, "You have answered rightly. Do this and you shall live."

But he, wanting to justify himself, said to Jesus, "And who is my neighbor?"

And Jesus answered and said, "A certain man went down from Jerusalem to
Jericho, and fell among thieves, who stripped him of his clothing, and wounded
him, and departed, leaving him half dead. And by chance there came down that
way a certain priest. And when he saw him, he passed by on the other side. And

likewise a Levite, when he was at the place, came and looked at him and passed by on the other side.

## "A Certain Samaritan. . .Had Compassion"

"But a certain Samaritan, as he journeyed, came where he was. And when he saw him, he had compassion on him, and went to him, and bound up his wounds, pouring in oil and wine, and sat him on his own beast, and brought him to an inn, and took care of him.

"And on the next day, when he departed, he took out two pence and gave them to the host, and said to him, 'Take care of him. And whatever more you spend, when I come again, I will repay you.' Now which of these three do you think was neighbor to him who fell among the thieves?"

And he said, "He who showed mercy to him."

Then Jesus said to him, "Go and do likewise." *Luke 10:25–37*

## 134. A VISIT WITH MARY AND MARTHA

Now it came to pass as they [Jesus and His disciples] went, that He entered into a certain village. And a certain woman named Martha received Him into her house. And she had a sister called Mary, who also sat at Jesus' feet and heard His word.

Jesus talks with the sisters Mary and Martha at their home in Bethany.

But Martha was troubled about much serving and came to Him and said, "Lord, do You not care that my sister has left me to serve alone? Therefore tell her to help me."

And Jesus answered and said to her, "Martha, Martha, you are anxious and troubled about many things. But one thing is needed, and Mary has chosen that good part, which shall not be taken away from her." *Luke 10:38–42*

## 135. REACHING OUT TO GOD THROUGH PRAYER

And it came to pass, that, as He [Jesus] was praying in a certain place, when He ceased, one of His disciples said to Him, "Lord, teach us to pray, as John also taught his disciples."

And He said to them, "When you pray, say:
Our Father who is in heaven,
Hallowed be Your name.
Your kingdom come.
Your will be done,
as in heaven, so on earth.
Give us day by day our daily bread.
And forgive us our sins,
for we also forgive everyone who is indebted to us.
And do not lead us into temptation,
but deliver us from evil."

And He said to them, "Which of you shall have a friend, and shall go to him at midnight and say to him, 'Friend, lend me three loaves, for a friend of mine has come to me in his journey, and I have nothing to set before him'; and from within he shall answer and say, 'Do not trouble me; the door is now shut, and my children are with me in bed; I cannot rise and give you anything'?

"I say to you, though he will not rise and give to him because he is his friend, yet because of his persistence he will rise and give him as many as he needs.

### "Seek, and You Shall Find"

"And I say to you, ask, and it shall be given to you; seek, and you shall find; knock, and it shall be opened to you. For everyone who asks receives, and he who seeks finds, and to him who knocks it shall be opened.

"If a son asks for bread from any of you who is a father, will he give him a stone? Or if he asks for a fish, will he give him a serpent instead of a fish? Or if he asks for an egg, will he offer him a scorpion?

"If you then, being evil, know how to give good gifts to your children, how much more shall your heavenly Father give the Holy Spirit to those who ask Him?" *Luke 11:1–13*

## 136. A HARSH ASSESSMENT OF THE PHARISEES

And as He [Jesus] spoke, a certain Pharisee begged Him to dine with him. And He went in and sat down at the table. And when the Pharisee saw it, he marveled that He had not first washed before dinner.

And the Lord said to him, "Now you Pharisees make the outside of the cup and the platter clean, but your inside is full of greed and wickedness. You fools! Didn't He who made what is outside also make what is inside? But rather give to the poor of such things as you have, and behold, all things are clean to you.

"But woe to you, Pharisees! For you tithe mint and rue and all manner of herbs, and pass over judgment and the love of God. You ought to have done these, and not left the other undone. Woe to you, Pharisees! For you love the best seats in the synagogues and greetings in the markets. Woe to you, scribes and Pharisees, hypocrites! For you are as unmarked graves, and the men who walk over them are not aware of them." *Luke 11:37–44*

And as He said these things to them, the scribes and the Pharisees began to urge Him vehemently, and to provoke Him to speak of many things, lying in wait for Him, and seeking to catch something out of His mouth, that they might accuse Him. *Luke 11:53–54*

## 137. PARABLE OF THE RICH LANDOWNER

And one of the company said to Him [Jesus], "Master, speak to my brother, that he would divide the inheritance with me."

And He said to him, "Man, who made Me a judge or a divider over you?" And He said to them, "Be careful and beware of covetousness, for a man's life does not consist in the abundance of the things that he possesses."

And He spoke a parable to them, saying, "The ground of a certain rich man brought forth plentifully. And he thought within himself, saying, 'What shall I do, because I have no room to store my fruits?' And he said, 'I will do this: I will pull down my barns and build greater ones, and there I will store all my fruits and my goods. And I will say to my soul, "Soul, you have many goods laid up for many years. Take your ease, eat, drink, and be merry.'"

"But God said to him, 'You fool. This night your soul shall be required of you. Then whose shall those things be that you have provided?' So is he who lays up treasure for himself and is not rich toward God." *Luke 12:13–21*

Wild flowers in northern Israel recall Jesus' teachings about His loving care for His followers.

## 138. PUT GOD'S KINGDOM FIRST

And He [Jesus] said to His disciples, "Therefore I say to you, do not worry about your life, what you shall eat, nor for the body, what you shall put on. Life is more than food, and the body is more than clothing. Consider the ravens, for they neither sow nor reap; they have neither storehouse nor barn, and God feeds them. How much more are you worth than the fowls?

"And which of you by worrying can add one cubit to his stature? If you then are not able to do that thing that is least, why do you worry about the rest?

"Consider the lilies, how they grow: they do not toil; they do not spin. And yet I say to you that Solomon in all his glory was not arrayed like one of these. If then God so clothes the grass, which today is in the field and tomorrow is cast into the oven, how much more will He clothe you, O you of little faith?

"And do not seek what you shall eat or what you shall drink, nor be of doubtful mind. For the nations of the world seek after all these things, and your Father knows that you have need of these things. But rather seek the kingdom of God, and all these things shall be added to you.

"Do not fear, little flock, for it is your Father's good pleasure to give you the kingdom. Sell what you have, and give to charity. Provide yourselves bags that do not grow old, a treasure in the heavens that does not fail, where no thief approaches, nor moth corrupts. For where your treasure is, there your heart will be also." *Luke 12:22–34*

## 139. AWARENESS OF JESUS' SECOND COMING

[Jesus said]: "Let your loins be girded about and your lights burning. And you yourselves be like men who wait for their master, when he will return from the wedding, that when he comes and knocks, they may open to him immediately. Blessed are those servants whom the master, when he comes, shall find watching.

"Truly I say to you that he shall gird himself and make them to sit down at the table, and will come forth and serve them. And if he comes in the second watch, or comes in the third watch, and finds them so, those servants are blessed.

### "You Also Be Ready"

"And know this, that if the master of the house had known what hour the thief would come, he would have watched and not have allowed his house to be broken into. Therefore you also be ready, for the Son of Man is coming at an hour when you do not think He will."

Then Peter said to Him, "Lord, do You speak this parable to us, or even to all?"

And the Lord said, "Who then is that faithful and wise steward, whom his master shall make ruler over his household, to give them their portion of food in due season? Blessed is that servant whom his master shall find so doing when he comes. Truly, I say to you that he will make him ruler over all that he has.

"But if that servant says in his heart, 'My master delays his coming,' and begins to beat the menservants and maidens, and to eat and drink and to be drunk, the master of that servant will come on a day when he does not look for him, and at an hour when he is not aware, and will cut him in pieces and will appoint him his portion with the unbelievers.

"And that servant who knew his master's will, and did not prepare himself or do according to his will, shall be beaten with many lashes. But he who did not know and committed things worthy of lashes shall be beaten with few lashes. For to whomever much is given, from him much shall be required. And to whom men have committed much, they will ask the more of him." *Luke 12:35–48*

## 140. PARABLE OF THE FRUITLESS FIG TREE

There were some present at that time who told Him [Jesus] of the Galileans whose blood Pilate had mingled with their sacrifices. And Jesus answered and said to them, "Do you suppose that these Galileans were sinners above all the other Galileans because they suffered such things? No, I tell you. But unless you repent, you shall all likewise perish.

"Or those eighteen on whom the tower in Siloam fell and slew them, do you think that they were sinners above all men who dwelled in Jerusalem? No, I tell you. But unless you repent, you shall all likewise perish."

He also spoke this parable: "A certain man had a fig tree planted in his vineyard, and he came and sought fruit on it and found none. Then he said to the caretaker of his vineyard, 'Behold, these three years I have come seeking fruit on this fig tree and find none. Cut it down. Why does it use up the ground?'

"And he answered and said to him, 'Lord, leave it alone this year also, till I shall dig about it and put dung on it. And if it bears fruit, well. And if not, then after that you shall cut it down.'" *Luke 13:1–9*

### ONE MORE CHANCE

This parable of a barren fruit tree (see section 140) referred to the nation of Israel. The Lord had given the Jewish people many opportunities to serve as His representative to the rest of the world. Instead, they became haughty and proud, insisting that they alone were worthy of God's love and salvation.

The Lord was giving Israel a second chance. If they accepted Jesus as His messenger of love to all the world, they would continue to enjoy God's favor. But if they continued in their pride and unbelief, they would lose their position as His chosen people.

## 141. A DISABLED WOMAN HEALED

And He [Jesus] was teaching in one of the synagogues on the Sabbath. And behold, there was a woman who had a spirit of infirmity eighteen years, and was bent over and could in no way lift herself up. And when Jesus saw her, He called her to Himself and said to her, "Woman, you are released from your infirmity." And He laid His hands on her, and immediately she was made straight and glorified God.

And the ruler of the synagogue answered with indignation because Jesus had healed on the Sabbath day. And he said to the people, "There are six days in which men ought to work. Therefore, come and be healed on them, and not on the Sabbath day."

The Lord then answered Him and said, "You hypocrite! Does not each one of you on the Sabbath untie his ox or his donkey from the stall and lead him away to watering? And ought not this woman, being a daughter of Abraham, whom Satan has bound, behold, these eighteen years, be released from this bond on the Sabbath day?"

And when He had said these things, all His adversaries were ashamed. And all the people rejoiced for all the glorious things that were done by Him. *Luke 13:10–17*

## 142. JESUS' ONENESS WITH GOD THE FATHER

And it was the Feast of the Dedication in Jerusalem, and it was winter. And Jesus walked in the temple in Solomon's porch. Then the Jews came around Him and said to Him, "How long do You make us to doubt? If You are the Christ, tell us plainly."

Jesus answered them, "I told you, and you do not believe. The works that I do in My Father's name, they bear witness of Me. But you do not believe because you are not of My sheep, as I said to you.

"My sheep hear My voice, and I know them, and they follow Me. And I give eternal life to them, and they shall never perish, nor shall any man pluck them out of My hand. My Father, who gave them to Me, is greater than all. And no man is able to pluck them out of My Father's hand. My Father and I are one."

### "For Which of Those Works Do You Stone Me?"

Then the Jews took up stones again to stone Him. Jesus answered them, "I have shown you many good works from My Father. For which of those works do you stone Me?"

The Jews answered Him, saying, "For a good work we do not stone You, but for blasphemy, and because You, being a man, make Yourself God."

Jesus answered them, "Is it not written in your Law, 'I said, "You are gods?"' If He called them gods, to whom the word of God came (and the scripture cannot be broken), do you say of Him whom the Father has sanctified and sent into the world, 'You are blaspheming,' because I said, 'I am the Son of God'?

"If I do not do the works of My Father, do not believe Me. But if I do, though you do not believe Me, believe the works, that you may know and believe that the Father is in Me and I in Him." *John 10:22–38*

# CHAPTER 9

## Jesus' Ministry in the Region Beyond the Jordan River

*Experiencing strong opposition in Jerusalem, Jesus withdrew with His disciples into a Gentile territory known as Perea, or "beyond Jordan." From here He traveled to Bethany, a village near Jerusalem, to raise His friend Lazarus from the dead. This enraged the religious leaders, who began to plot His death.*

## 143. WITHDRAWAL WITH THE TWELVE

Therefore they [Pharisees] sought again to take Him [Jesus], but He escaped out of their hand and went away again beyond the Jordan to the place where John at first baptized, and there He remained.

And many came to Him and said, "John did no miracle, but all things that John spoke of this man were true." And many believed in Him there. *John 10:39–42*

## 144. JESUS LAMENTS JERUSALEM'S UNBELIEF

The same day some of the Pharisees came, saying to Him [Jesus], "Get out and depart from here, for Herod will kill You."

And He said to them, "Go, and tell that fox, 'Behold, I cast out demons and I do cures today and tomorrow, and the third day I shall be perfected.' Nevertheless I must walk today, and tomorrow, and the day following. For it cannot be that a prophet perishes outside Jerusalem.

"O Jerusalem, Jerusalem, who kills the prophets, and stones those who are sent to you. How often I would have gathered your children together, as a hen gathers her brood under her wings, and you would not!

A mother hen protecting her chicks recalls Jesus' lament about His enemies in Jerusalem.

"Behold, your house is left to you desolate. And truly I say to you, you shall not see Me until the time comes when you shall say, 'Blessed is He who comes in the name of the Lord.'" *Luke 13:31–35*

SEE PARALLEL ACCOUNT AT MATTHEW 23:37–39

## 145. HEALING OF A MAN WITH BODY FLUID

And it came to pass, as He [Jesus] went into the house of one of the chief Pharisees to eat bread on the Sabbath day, that they watched Him. And, behold, there was a certain man before Him who had the dropsy. And Jesus, answering, spoke to the lawyers and Pharisees, saying, "Is it lawful to heal on the Sabbath day?"

And they remained silent. And He took him and healed him, and let him go. And He answered them, saying, "Which of you shall have a donkey or an ox that has fallen into a pit, and will not immediately pull him out on the Sabbath day?"

And again they could not answer Him for these things. *Luke 14:1–6*

## 146. SEEK THE LOWEST PLACE

And He [Jesus] put forth a parable to those who were invited, when He observed how they chose the places of honor, saying to them: "When you are invited by any man to a wedding, do not sit down in the place of honor, lest a more honorable man than you be invited by him, and he who invited you and him come and say to you, 'Give this man place,' and with shame you begin to take the lowest place.

"But when you are invited, go and sit down in the lowest place, that when he who invited you comes, he may say to you, 'Friend, go up higher.' Then you shall have honor in the presence of those who sit at the table with you. For whoever exalts himself shall be humbled, and he who humbles himself shall be exalted."

Then He also said to him who invited him, "When you make a dinner or a supper, do not call your friends or your brothers, or your relatives or your rich neighbors, lest they also invite you back and a recompense be made to you.

"But when you make a feast, call the poor, the maimed, the lame, the blind. And you shall be blessed, for they cannot repay you. For you shall be repaid at the resurrection of the just." *Luke 14:7–14*

## 147. PARABLE OF THE REFUSED INVITATIONS

And when one of those who sat at the table with Him heard these things, he said to Him, "Blessed is he who shall eat bread in the kingdom of God."

Then He said to him, "A certain man made a great supper and invited many, and sent his servant at suppertime to say to those who were invited, 'Come, for all things are now ready.' And they all with one consent began to make excuses.

"The first said to him, 'I have bought a piece of ground, and I need to go and see it. I ask you to have me excused.' And another said, 'I have bought five yoke of oxen, and I am going to test them. I ask you to have me excused.' And another said, 'I have married a wife, and therefore I cannot come.'

"So that servant came and told his master these things. Then the master of the house, being angry, said to his servant, 'Go out quickly into the streets and lanes of the city, and bring in here the poor, and the maimed, and the lame, and the blind.'

### THE IN-CROWD AND THE HAVE-NOTS

Jesus had the Pharisees in mind when He told this parable about people who turned down a generous man's invitation (see section 147). Their self-righteousness and opposition to Jesus kept them from enjoying God's lavish feast of abundant life that He offered to everyone. But the outcasts of society—those who turned in faith to Jesus—were partaking of the festivities that the Pharisees had turned down.

"And the servant said, 'Lord, it is done as you have commanded, and yet there is room.'

"And the master said to the servant, 'Go out into the highways and hedges, and compel them to come in, that my house may be filled. For I say to you that none of those men who were invited shall taste of my supper.'" *Luke 14:15–24*

Poor, disabled, and outcast people replace those who refused Jesus' invitation to the wedding feast.

## 148. COUNTING THE COST OF DISCIPLESHIP

And great multitudes went with Him [Jesus]. And He turned and said to them, "If any man comes to Me and does not hate his father, and mother, and wife, and children, and brothers, and sisters, yes, and also his own life, he cannot be My disciple. And whoever does not bear his cross and come after Me cannot be My disciple.

"For which of you intending to build a tower does not sit down first and count the cost, whether he has enough to finish it? Perhaps after he has laid the foundation and is not able to finish it, all who see it begin to mock him, saying, 'This man began to build and was not able to finish.'

"Or what king going to make war against another king does not sit down first and consult whether he is able with ten thousand to meet him who comes against him with twenty thousand? Or else, while the other is still a great way off, he sends a delegation and desires conditions of peace. So likewise, whoever of you who does not forsake all that he has cannot be My disciple.

"Salt is good, but if the salt has lost its taste, with what shall it be seasoned? It is neither fit for the land nor for the dunghill, but men cast it out. He who has ears to hear, let him hear." *Luke 14:25–35*

## 149. PARABLE OF THE LOST SHEEP

Then all the tax collectors and sinners drew near to Him [ Jesus] to hear Him. And the Pharisees and scribes murmured, saying, "This man receives sinners and eats with them."

And He spoke this parable to them, saying: "What man of you, having a hundred sheep, if he loses one of them, does not leave the ninety-nine in the wilderness and go after what is lost until he finds it? And when he has found it, he lays it on his shoulders, rejoicing. And when he comes home, he calls together his friends and neighbors, saying to them, 'Rejoice with me, for I have found my sheep that was lost.'

"I say to you that likewise there shall be more joy in heaven over one sinner who repents than over ninety-nine righteous people who need no repentance." *Luke 15:1–7*

See parallel account at Matthew 18:12–14

Jesus' parable of the lost sheep described God's joy at sinners who come to repentance.

## 150. PARABLE OF THE LOST COIN

[Jesus said]: "Or what woman, having ten pieces of silver, if she loses one piece, does not light a candle, and sweep the house, and seek diligently till she finds it? And when she has found it, she calls her friends and her neighbors together, saying, 'Rejoice with me, for I have found the piece that I had lost.'

"Likewise, I say to you, there is joy in the presence of the angels of God over one sinner who repents." *Luke 15:8–10*

### HOPE FOR THE LOST

The account of a lost sheep is the first of three back-to-back parables from Luke's Gospel (see sections 149–151). Jesus directed these parables to the Pharisees, who were criticizing Him for associating with sinners.

With these parables, Jesus served notice that He was sent to call the lost and hopeless to repentance and salvation. His inclusive attitude was similar to that of the loving father, who welcomed his wayward son back home.

By contrast, the Pharisees were like the lost son's older brother. He thought the boy did not deserve to be welcomed back with such open-armed acceptance and a lavish family celebration. But his father replied, "It was fitting that we should make merry and be glad, for this your brother was dead and is alive again, and was lost and is found" (Luke 15:32).

## 151. PARABLE OF THE LOST SON

And He [Jesus] said, "A certain man had two sons. And the younger of them said to his father, 'Father, give me the portion of goods that falls to me.' And he divided his wealth between them.

"And not many days after, the younger son gathered everything together, and took his journey into a far country, and there wasted his substance with wasteful living. And when he had spent all, there arose a mighty famine in that land, and he began to be in need.

"And he went and hired himself to a citizen of that country, and he sent him into his fields to feed swine. And he would willingly have filled his belly with the husks that the swine ate, and no man gave anything to him.

"And when he came to himself, he said, 'How many of my father's hired servants have enough bread, and to spare, and I perish with hunger! I will arise and go to my father and will say to him, "Father, I have sinned against heaven and before you and am no longer worthy to be called your son. Make me as one of your hired servants."'

### "His Father. . .Had Compassion"

"And he arose and came to his father. But when he was still a great way off, his father saw him and had compassion, and ran and fell on his neck and kissed him. And the son said to him, 'Father, I have sinned against heaven and in your sight and am no longer worthy to be called your son.'

"But the father said to his servants, 'Bring forth the best robe and put it on him, and put a ring on his hand and shoes on his feet. And bring the fatted calf here and kill it, and let us eat and be merry. For this my son was dead and is alive again. He was lost and is found.' And they began to be merry.

In Jesus' parable, a wayward son receives a warm welcome from his loving father.

"Now his elder son was in the field. And as he came and drew near to the house, he heard music and dancing. And he called one of the servants and asked what these things meant. And he said to him, 'Your brother has come, and your father has killed the fatted calf because he has received him safe and sound.'

## "You Never Gave Me a Young Goat"

"And he was angry and would not go in. Therefore his father came out and entreated him. And he answered and said to his father, 'Look, these many years I have served you, I never transgressed your commandment at any time. And yet you never gave me a young goat, that I might make merry with my friends. But as soon as this your son came, who has devoured your wealth with harlots, you have killed the fatted calf for him.'

"And he said to him, 'Son, you are always with me, and all that I have is yours. It was fitting that we should make merry and be glad, for this your brother was dead and is alive again, and was lost and is found.'" *Luke 15:11–32*

# 152. PARABLE OF THE SHREWD MANAGER

And He [Jesus] also said to His disciples, "There was a certain rich man who had a steward, and an accusation was made of him that he had wasted his goods. And he called him and said to him, 'How is it that I hear this of you? Give an account of your stewardship, for you may no longer be steward.'

"Then the steward said within himself, 'What shall I do? For my master is taking away the stewardship from me. I cannot dig; I am ashamed to beg. I have resolved what to do, that when I am put out of the stewardship, they may receive me into their houses.'

"So he called every one of his master's debtors to him and said to the first, 'How much do you owe to my master?'

"And he said, 'A hundred measures of oil.'

"And he said to him, 'Take your bill, and sit down quickly and write fifty.'

"Then he said to another, 'And how much do you owe?'

"And he said, 'A hundred measures of wheat.'

"And he said to him, 'Take your bill, and write eighty.'

## "Wiser. . .than the Children of Light"

"And the master commended the unjust steward because he had done wisely. For the children of this world are wiser in their generation than the children of light.

"And I say to you, make friends for yourselves by the riches of unrighteousness, that when you fail, they may receive you into everlasting habitations. He who is faithful in what is least is also faithful in much, and he who is unjust in the least is also unjust in much.

"Therefore if you have not been faithful in the unrighteous riches, who will commit the true riches to your trust? And if you have not been faithful in what is another man's, who shall give you what is your own?

"No servant can serve two masters. For either he will hate the one and love the other, or else he will hold to the one and despise the other. You cannot serve God and riches." *Luke 16:1–13*

## 153. PARABLE OF A RICH MAN AND A POOR MAN

[Jesus said]: "There was a certain rich man who was clothed in purple and fine linen and feasted sumptuously every day. And there was a certain beggar named Lazarus, full of sores, who was laid at his gate, and desired to be fed with the crumbs that fell from the rich man's table. Moreover the dogs came and licked his sores.

"And it came to pass that the beggar died and was carried by the angels into Abraham's bosom. The rich man also died and was buried. And being in torment in hell, he lifted up his eyes and saw Abraham afar off, and Lazarus in his bosom.

### "Father Abraham, Have Mercy"

"And he cried and said, 'Father Abraham, have mercy on me, and send Lazarus that he may dip the tip of his finger in water and cool my tongue, for I am tormented in this flame.'

"But Abraham said, 'Son, remember that in your lifetime you received your good things, and likewise Lazarus evil things. But now he is comforted and you are tormented. And besides all this, between us and you there is a great chasm fixed, so that those who would pass from here to you cannot, nor can those who would come from there pass to us.'

"Then he said, 'I ask you, therefore, father, that you would send him to my father's house, for I have five brothers, that he may testify to them, lest they also come into this place of torment.'

"Abraham said to him, 'They have Moses and the prophets. Let them hear them.'

### THE GREAT SEPARATION

The contrast in this parable (see section 153) could not be greater—a rich man with all the world's goods and a poor man who had to beg for scraps of food. But all this changed when both men died. The rich man in Hades became the beggar, while the poor man enjoyed the good life in paradise.

The two were separated by a gap that could not be bridged. This shows that the choices they made while on earth had eternal consequences. Beware, Jesus declared: A life lived only for oneself will result in separation from God, in both this life and the life to come.

"And he said, 'No, father Abraham. But if one went to them from the dead, they will repent.'

"And he said to him, 'If they do not hear Moses and the prophets, they will not be persuaded if one rises from the dead.'" *Luke 16:19–31*

In Jesus' parable, a beggar named Lazarus asks for a handout from a rich man.

## 154. TEACHINGS ON FAITH AND DUTY

And the apostles said to the Lord, "Increase our faith."

And the Lord said, "If you had faith as a grain of mustard seed, you might say to this mulberry tree, 'Be plucked up by the roots and be planted in the sea,' and it would obey you.

"But which of you, having a servant plowing or feeding cattle, will say to him right away when he has come from the field, 'Go and sit down at the table'? And will he not rather say to him, 'Prepare something that I may eat, and gird yourself, and serve me till I have eaten and drunk, and afterward you shall eat and drink'?

"Does he thank that servant because he did the things that were commanded him? I think not. So likewise you, when you shall have done all those things that are commanded of you, say, 'We are unprofitable servants. We have done what was our duty to do.'" *Luke 17:5–10*

## 155. A SERIOUS ILLNESS STRIKES LAZARUS

Now a certain man was sick, named Lazarus of Bethany, the town of Mary and her sister Martha. It was that Mary who anointed the Lord with ointment and wiped His feet with her hair, whose brother Lazarus was sick. Therefore his sisters sent to Him, saying, "Lord, behold, he whom You love is sick."

When Jesus heard that, He said, "This sickness is not to death, but for the glory of God, that the Son of God might be glorified by it." Now Jesus loved Martha and her sister and Lazarus. Therefore when He had heard that he was sick, He remained two days still in the same place where He was. Then after that He said to His disciples, "Let us go into Judea again."

His disciples said to Him, "Master, lately the Jews have sought to stone You, and You are going there again?"

### "I Go [to] Awake [Lazarus] Out of Sleep"

Jesus answered, "Are there not twelve hours in the day? If any man walks in the day, he does not stumble because he sees the light of this world. But if a man walks in the night, he stumbles because there is no light in him." He said these things, and after that He said to them, "Our friend Lazarus sleeps. But I go that I may awake him out of sleep."

Then His disciples said, "Lord, if he sleeps, he shall do well." However, Jesus spoke of his death, but they thought that He had spoken of taking rest in sleep.

Then said Jesus to them plainly, "Lazarus is dead. And I am glad for your sakes that I was not there, so that you may believe. Nevertheless let us go to him."

Then Thomas, who is called Didymus, said to his fellow disciples, "Let us also go, that we may die with Him." *John 11:1–16*

## 156. JESUS WEEPS WITH THE SISTERS OF LAZARUS

Then when Jesus came [to Bethany], He found that he [Lazarus] had already been laying in the grave four days. Now Bethany was near to Jerusalem, about fifteen furlongs off. And many of the Jews came to Martha and Mary to comfort them concerning their brother.

Then Martha, as soon as she heard that Jesus was coming, went and met Him, but Mary still sat in the house. Then Martha said to Jesus, "Lord, if You had been here, my brother would not have died. But even now I know that whatever You will ask of God, God will give it You."

Jesus said to her, "Your brother shall rise again."

Martha said to Him, "I know that he shall rise again in the resurrection on the last day."

## "I Am the Resurrection and the Life"

Jesus said to her, "I am the resurrection and the life. He who believes in Me, though he were dead, yet shall he live. And whoever lives and believes in Me shall never die. Do you believe this?"

She said to Him, "Yes, Lord, I believe that You are the Christ, the Son of God, who is coming into the world." And when she had said this, she went her way and called Mary her sister secretly, saying, "The Master has come and calls for you." As soon as she heard that, she arose quickly and came to Him.

Now Jesus had not yet come into the town, but was in that place where Martha met Him. Then the Jews who were with her and comforted her in the house, when they saw Mary, that she rose up hastily and went out, followed her, saying, "She goes to the grave to weep there."

Then when Mary had come where Jesus was and saw Him, she fell down at His feet, saying to Him, "Lord, if You had been here, my brother would not have died."

Therefore when Jesus saw her weeping, and the Jews who came with her also weeping, He groaned in the spirit and was troubled, and said, "Where have you laid him?"

They said to Him, "Lord, come and see."

Jesus wept. Then the Jews said, "Behold how He loved him!"

And some of them said, "Could not this man, who opened the eyes of the blind, have caused that even this man should not have died?" *John 11:17–37*

## 157. LAZARUS RAISED FROM THE DEAD

Therefore Jesus, again groaning in Himself, came to the grave. It was a cave, and a stone lay on it. Jesus said, "Take away the stone."

Martha, the sister of him who was dead, said to Him, "Lord, by this time he stinks, for he has been dead four days."

Jesus said to her, "Did I not say to you that if you would believe you should see the glory of God?" Then they took away the stone from the place where the dead was laid. And Jesus lifted up His eyes and said, "Father, I thank You that You have heard Me. And I knew that You always hear Me, but because of the people who stand by I said it, that they may believe that You have sent Me."

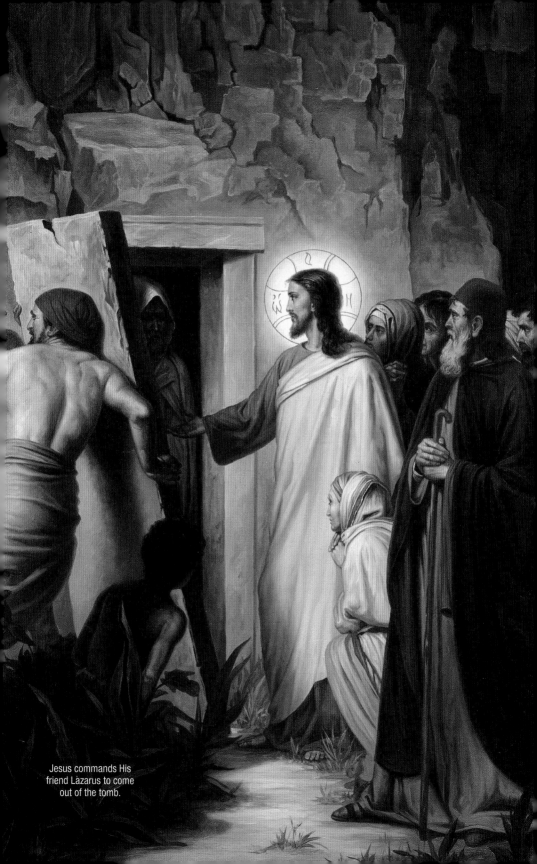

Jesus commands His friend Lazarus to come out of the tomb.

And thus when He had spoken, He cried with a loud voice, "Lazarus, come out!" And he who was dead came out, bound hand and foot with grave clothes, and his face was bound about with a cloth. Jesus said to them, "Unbind him, and let him go." *John 11:38–44*

## AWAY WITH JESUS AND LAZARUS

Jesus' raising of Lazarus (see section 157) sealed His fate. The Jewish high court, known as the council or Sanhedrin, launched a plan to arrest Him and have Him put to death (see section 158). They rationalized that Jesus' actions would cause a disturbance that would bring the Roman army down on their heads. But the real reason for their hatred was jealousy. Jesus' claim to be God's divine agent was a threat to their authority.

The Sanhedrin even threatened to include Lazarus in their death plot. His spectacular raising had caused many people to believe in Jesus (see section 172).

## 158. RELIGIOUS LEADERS PLOT JESUS' DEATH

Then many of the Jews who came to Mary and had seen the things that Jesus did believed in Him. But some of them went their ways to the Pharisees and told them what things Jesus had done.

Then the chief priests and the Pharisees gathered a council and said, "What do we do? For this man does many miracles. Thus if we leave Him alone, all men will believe in Him, and the Romans shall come and take away both our place and nation."

And one of them, named Caiaphas, being the high priest that same year, said to them, "You know nothing at all, nor consider that it is expedient for us that one man should die for the people, and that the whole nation should not perish."

And he spoke this not of himself. But being high priest that year he prophesied that Jesus would die for that nation, and not for that nation only, but also that He would gather together in one the children of God who were scattered abroad.

Then from that day forth, they took counsel together to put Him to death. Therefore Jesus no longer walked openly among the Jews but went from there to a country near the wilderness, into a city called Ephraim, and stayed there with His disciples. *John 11:45–54*

## 159. TEN MEN WITH LEPROSY HEALED

And it came to pass, as He [Jesus] went to Jerusalem, that He passed through the midst of Samaria and Galilee. And as He entered into a certain village, ten men who were lepers, who stood afar off, met Him. And they lifted up their voices and said, "Jesus, Master, have mercy on us."

And when He saw them, He said to them, "Go show yourselves to the priests."

And it came to pass, that as they went, they were cleansed.

And one of them, when he saw that he was healed, turned back, and with a loud voice glorified God, and fell down on his face at His feet, giving Him thanks. And he was a Samaritan.

And Jesus answered and said, "Were there not ten cleansed? But where are the nine? There are none found who returned to give glory to God, save this foreigner." And He said to him, "Arise, go your way. Your faith has healed you." *Luke 17:11–19*

# 160. THE KINGDOM OF GOD AND JESUS' RETURN

And when He [Jesus] was questioned by the Pharisees when the kingdom of God should come, He answered them and said, "The kingdom of God does not come with observation, nor shall they say, 'Look here!' or 'Look there!' For behold, the kingdom of God is within you."

And He said to the disciples, "The days will come when you shall desire to see one of the days of the Son of Man, and you shall not see it. And they shall say to you, 'Look here' or 'Look there.' Do not go after them or follow them. For as the lightning that flashes out of the one part under heaven shines to the other part under heaven, so also shall the Son of Man be in His day.

"But first He must suffer many things and be rejected by this generation. And as it was in the days of Noah, so shall it also be in the days of the Son of Man. They ate, they drank, they married wives, they were given in marriage, until the day that Noah entered into the ark and the flood came and destroyed them all.

"Likewise as it was also in the days of Lot: they ate, they drank, they bought, they sold, they planted, they built. But the same day that Lot went out of Sodom it rained fire and brimstone from heaven and destroyed them all. It shall be this way on the day when the Son of Man is revealed." *Luke 17:20–30*

Jesus' return will occur as quickly as a flash of lightning during a storm.

## 161. PARABLE OF THE PERSISTENT WIDOW

And He [Jesus] spoke a parable to them to this end, that men ought always to pray and not to faint, saying, "In a city there was a judge who did not fear God or regard man. And there was a widow in that city, and she came to him, saying, 'Take vengeance on my adversary.' And he would not for a while.

"But afterward he said within himself, 'Though I do not fear God or regard man, yet because this widow troubles me I will avenge her, lest by her continual coming she wearies me.'"

And the Lord said, "Hear what the unjust judge said. And shall not God avenge His own elect, who cry day and night to Him, though He bears long with them? I tell you that He will avenge them speedily. Nevertheless, when the Son of Man comes, shall He find faith on the earth?" *Luke 18:1–8*

## 162. PARABLE OF THE SELF-RIGHTEOUS PHARISEE

And He [Jesus] spoke this parable to some who trusted in themselves that they were righteous, and despised others: "Two men went up into the temple to pray, the one a Pharisee and the other a tax collector. The Pharisee stood by himself and prayed this: 'God, I thank You that I am not as other men are—extortioners, unjust, adulterers, or even as this tax collector. I fast twice in the week. I give tithes of all that I possess.'

### THE PERIL OF PRIDE

It's a stretch to call the Pharisee's words in this parable a prayer (see section 162). He addressed his remarks to himself—a prideful rehearsal of his good deeds. By contrast, the tax collector recognized his sins, and confessed them to God in a spirit of repentance.

Pride blinds us to our own sins and causes us to think we are not so bad when weighed against the wrongdoing of others. But humble recognition of our unworthiness leads us to seek the grace and mercy of God.

"And the tax collector, standing afar off, would not so much as lift up his eyes to heaven, but struck his breast, saying, 'God, be merciful to me, a sinner.' I tell you, this man went down to his house justified rather than the other. For everyone who exalts himself shall be humbled, and he who humbles himself shall be exalted." *Luke 18:9–14*

In Jesus' parable, a penitent tax collector rather than a prideful Pharisee received God's commendation.

## 163. A QUESTION ABOUT DIVORCE

And it came to pass that when Jesus had finished these sayings, He departed from Galilee and came into the region of Judea beyond the Jordan. And great multitudes followed Him, and He healed them there.

The Pharisees also came to Him, tempting Him, and saying to Him, "Is it lawful for a man to divorce his wife for any reason?"

And He answered and said to them, "Have you not read that He who made them at the beginning 'made them male and female' and said, 'For this reason a man shall leave father and mother and shall cling to his wife, and they two shall be one flesh'? Therefore they are no more two, but one flesh. Therefore what God has joined together, let no man separate."

They said to Him, "Why then did Moses command to give a certificate of divorce and to send her away?"

## "From the Beginning It Was Not So"

He said to them, "Moses, because of the hardness of your hearts, allowed you to divorce your wives, but from the beginning it was not so. And I say to you, whoever divorces his wife, except for fornication, and marries another commits adultery. And whoever marries her who is divorced commits adultery."

His disciples said to Him, "If the case of the man with his wife is so, it is good not to marry."

But He said to them, "All men cannot receive this saying, except those to whom it is given. For there are some eunuchs who were so born from their mother's womb, and there are some eunuchs who were made eunuchs by men, and there are eunuchs who have made themselves eunuchs for the kingdom of heaven's sake. He who is able to receive it, let him receive it." *Matthew 19:1–12*

SEE PARALLEL ACCOUNT AT MARK 10:1–12

Though His disciples tried to object, Jesus blessed children brought to Him by their parents.

## 164. A WELCOME FOR LITTLE CHILDREN

And they brought young children to Him, that He should touch them, and His disciples rebuked those who brought them. But when Jesus saw it, He was very displeased and said to them, "Allow the little children to come to Me, and do not forbid them, for of such is the kingdom of God. Truly I say to you, whoever shall not receive the kingdom of God as a little child, he shall not enter in it."

And He took them up in His arms, put His hands on them, and blessed them. *Mark 10:13–16*

SEE PARALLEL ACCOUNTS AT MATTHEW 19:13–15 AND LUKE 18:15–17

## 165. A QUESTION FROM A RICH YOUNG MAN

And behold, one came and said to Him, "Good Master, what good thing shall I do that I may have eternal life?" And He said to him, "Why do you call Me good? There is no one good but One—that is, God. But if you will enter into life, keep the commandments."

He said to Him, "Which ones?"

Jesus said, "You shall not murder. You shall not commit adultery. You shall not steal. You shall not bear false witness. Honor your father and your mother. And you shall love your neighbor as yourself."

The young man said to Him, "All these things I have kept from my youth. What do I still lack?"

Jesus said to Him, "If you want to be perfect, go and sell what you have and give to the poor, and you shall have treasure in heaven. And come and follow Me."

But when the young man heard that saying, he went away sorrowful, for he had great possessions.

Then Jesus said to His disciples, "Truly I say to you that it is difficult for a rich man to enter into the kingdom of heaven. And again I say to you, it is easier for a camel to go through the eye of a needle than for a rich man to enter into the kingdom of God."

When His disciples heard it, they were exceedingly amazed, saying, "Who then can be saved?"

But Jesus looked at them and said to them, "With men this is impossible, but with God all things are possible." *Matthew 19:16–26*

### A NAME FROM THREE SOURCES

Jesus' encounter with a wealthy young man (see section 165) is a good example of how the different Gospels enrich and support one another. Matthew's account tells us he was a "young man" (Matthew 19:20). Mark notes Jesus' observation that the man was rich (Mark 10:23). And Luke reports that he was "a ruler" (Luke 18:18). Thus the name by which he is known to students of the Bible: the rich young ruler.

Modern grape harvesters recall Jesus' parable about workers in a vineyard.

## 166. PARABLE OF HIRED VINEYARD WORKERS

[Jesus said]: "For the kingdom of heaven is similar to a man who was a landowner who went out early in the morning to hire laborers into his vineyard. And when he had agreed with the laborers for a penny a day, he sent them into his vineyard.

"And he went out about the third hour and saw others standing idle in the marketplace, and said to them, 'You go also into the vineyard, and whatever is right I will give you.' And they went their way. Again he went out about the sixth and ninth hour and did likewise.

"And about the eleventh hour he went out and found others standing idle, and said to them, 'Why do you stand here idle all the day?' They said to him, 'Because no man has hired us.' He said to them, 'You go also into the vineyard, and whatever is right, that you shall receive.'

### "Every Man Received a Penny"

"So when evening came, the lord of the vineyard said to his steward, 'Call the laborers and give them their wages, beginning from the last to the first.' And when those came who were hired about the eleventh hour, every man received a penny. But when the first came, they supposed that they should have received more. And likewise, every man received a penny.

"And when they had received it, they murmured against the master of the house, saying, 'These last men have worked but one hour, and you have made them equal to us who have borne the burden and heat of the day.'

"But he answered one of them and said, 'Friend, I did you no wrong. Did you not agree with me for a penny? Take what is yours and go your way. I want to give to this last man the same as to you. Is it not lawful for me to do what I want with my own? Is your eye evil because I am good?' So the last shall be first, and the first last. For many are called, but few chosen." *Matthew 20:1–16*

## 167. A BRASH REQUEST FROM JAMES AND JOHN

And James and John, the sons of Zebedee, came to Him [Jesus], saying, "Master, we want You to do for us whatever we desire."

And He said to them, "What do you want Me to do for you?"

They said to Him, "Grant to us that we may sit, one on Your right hand and the other on Your left hand, in Your glory."

But Jesus said to them, "You do not know what you ask. Can you drink of the cup that I drink of, and be baptized with the baptism that I am baptized with?"

And they said to Him, "We can."

And Jesus said to them, "You shall indeed drink of the cup that I drink of, and you shall be baptized with the baptism that I am baptized with, but to sit on My right hand and on My left hand is not Mine to give, but it shall be given to those for whom it is prepared." *Mark 10:35–40*

### A MOTHER'S DESIRE

Matthew's parallel account of this event (see section 167) has the mother of James and John making this request for her two sons (Matthew 20:20–23). Some interpreters believe she was Salome, the sister of Jesus' mother, Mary. If so, she may have assumed that Jesus would show favoritism to her sons because of this family relationship.

But the problem is that she and her sons were thinking in worldly terms. The kingdom of God that Jesus came to establish was not a place where people jockeyed for position; it was a spiritual fellowship where commitment to Jesus and His teachings left no room for human pride and selfish ambition.

## 168. A LESSON ON TRUE GREATNESS

And when the ten [other disciples of Jesus] heard it, they were moved with indignation against the two brothers. But Jesus called them to Himself and said, "You know that the princes of the Gentiles exercise dominion over them, and those who are great exercise authority over them.

"But it shall not be so among you. But whoever wants to be great among you, let him be your minister. And whoever wants to be chief among you, let him be your servant, even as the Son of Man came not to be ministered to but to minister and to give His life as a ransom for many." *Matthew 20:24–28*

SEE PARALLEL ACCOUNT AT MARK 10:41–45

## 169. BLIND BARTIMAEUS HEALED AT JERICHO

And they [Jesus and His disciples] came to Jericho. And as He went out of Jericho with His disciples and a great number of people, blind Bartimaeus, the son of Timaeus, sat begging by the highway. And when he heard that it was Jesus of Nazareth, he began to cry out and say, "Jesus, Son of David, have mercy on me!" And many charged him that he should remain silent, but he cried a great deal the more, "Son of David, have mercy on me!"

### SIGHT FOR THE BLIND

Accounts of this miraculous healing at Jericho also appear in Matthew (20:29–34) and Luke (18:35–43). According to Matthew, two unidentified blind men were healed by Jesus at this ancient city. Luke reports that one unidentified man was healed. Only Mark's Gospel records the man's name as Bartimaeus.

And Jesus stood still and commanded him to be called. And they called the blind man, saying to him, "Be of good comfort. Rise. He is calling you." And casting away his garment, he rose and came to Jesus.

And Jesus answered and said to him, "What do you want Me to do for you?"

The blind man said to Him, "Lord, that I might receive my sight."

And Jesus said to him, "Go your way. Your faith has made you well." And immediately he received his sight and followed Jesus on the road. *Mark 10:46–52*

## 170. A TAX COLLECTOR MEETS JESUS

And Jesus entered and passed through Jericho. And behold, there was a man named Zacchaeus, who was the chief among the tax collectors, and he was rich. And he sought to see who Jesus was, and could not for the crowd, because he was little in stature. And he ran ahead and climbed up into a sycamore tree to see Him, for He was to pass that way.

And when Jesus came to the place, He looked up and saw him, and said to him, "Zacchaeus, hurry and come down, for today I must stay at your house." And

In Jericho, Bartimaeus begs Jesus to restore his sight.

he hurried and came down, and received Him joyfully. And when they saw it, they all murmured, saying, "He has gone to be the guest of a man who is a sinner."

And Zacchaeus stood and said to the Lord, "Behold, Lord, half of my goods I give to the poor. And if I have taken anything from any man by false accusation, I restore him fourfold."

And Jesus said to him, "This day salvation has come to this house, because he also is a son of Abraham. For the Son of Man has come to seek and to save what was lost." *Luke 19:1–10*

From his perch in a tree, Zacchaeus waits to catch a glimpse of Jesus.

## 171. PARABLE OF THE POUNDS

And as they [the crowd] heard these things, He [Jesus] added and spoke a parable, because He was near to Jerusalem and because they thought that the kingdom of God should appear immediately.

Therefore He said: "A certain nobleman went into a far country to receive for himself a kingdom and to return. And he called his ten servants, and gave them ten pounds, and said to them, 'Make a profit till I come.' But his citizens hated him and sent a message after him, saying, 'We will not have this man to reign over us.'

"And it came to pass that when he returned, having received the kingdom, then he commanded these servants to be called to him, to whom he had given the money, that he might know how much every man had gained by trading.

"Then the first came, saying, 'Lord, your pound has gained ten pounds.' And he said to him, 'Well done, good servant. Because you have been faithful in very little, have authority over ten cities.'

"And the second came, saying, 'Lord, your pound has gained five pounds.' And likewise he said to him, 'You also be over five cities.'

## "Here Is Your Pound"

"And another came, saying, 'Lord, behold, here is your pound, which I have kept laid away in a handkerchief. For I feared you, because you are an austere man. You take up what you did not lay down and reap what you did not sow.'

"And he said to him, 'Out of your own mouth I will judge you, you wicked servant. You knew that I was an austere man, taking up what I had not laid down and reaping what I did not sow. Why then did you not put my money into the bank, that at my coming I might have claimed my own with interest?'

"And he said to those who stood by, 'Take from him the pound, and give it to him who has ten pounds.' (And they said to him, 'Lord, he has ten pounds.') 'For I say to you, that to everyone who has shall be given, and from him who does not have, even what he has shall be taken away from him. But bring here those enemies of mine, who did not want me to reign over them, and slay them before me.'"

And when He had said this, He went ahead, ascending to Jerusalem. *Luke 19:11–28*

# CHAPTER 10

# Events from the Triumphal Entry to the Garden of Gethsemane

*This chapter covers five days in Jesus' life—from His entry into Jerusalem on Palm Sunday to His struggle over His approaching death in the garden of Gethsemane on Maundy Thursday. Chapter 11 covers His arrest, trial, and crucifixion. These two chapters combined include the events known as Holy Week on the Christian calendar— the final week of Jesus' earthly ministry.*

## 172. JESUS ARRIVES AT BETHANY, NEAR JERUSALEM

And the Jews' Passover was near at hand, and many went out of the country up to Jerusalem before the Passover to purify themselves. Then they sought Jesus and spoke among themselves as they stood in the temple, "What do you think, that He will not come to the feast?"

Now both the chief priests and the Pharisees had given a commandment, that if any man knew where He was, he should reveal it, that they might take Him. Then, six days before the Passover, Jesus came to Bethany, where Lazarus was who had been dead, whom He raised from the dead. *John 11:55–12:1*

Therefore many people of the Jews knew that He was there, and they came not only for Jesus' sake but that they might also see Lazarus, whom He had raised from the dead. But the chief priests consulted that they might also put Lazarus to death, because on account of him many of the Jews went away and believed in Jesus. *John 12:9–11*

### A FAMILIAR PLACE

Jesus' arrival at Bethany (see section 172) set the stage for His final week in Jerusalem. Here He had raised his friend Lazarus from the dead just a few weeks before. During His ministry, Jesus often visited in the home of Lazarus and his two sisters, Mary and Martha, at this little town (see sections 134 and 173).

Bethany today is known by its Arabic name, el Azariyeh. Its most notable attraction is a gloomy cave said to be the tomb of Lazarus. The site is visited every year by thousands of Holy Land tourists.

## 173. MARY, SISTER OF LAZARUS, ANOINTS JESUS

Then Mary took a pound of very costly ointment of spikenard, and anointed the feet of Jesus, and wiped His feet with her hair. And the house was filled with the odor of the ointment.

Then one of His disciples, Judas Iscariot, Simon's son, who would betray Him, said, "Why was this ointment not sold for three hundred pence and given to the poor?" He said this, not that he cared for the poor, but because he was a thief, and had the bag, and bore what was put in it.

Then Jesus said, "Leave her alone. She has kept this in preparation for the day of My burial. For the poor you always have with you, but you do not always have Me." *John 12:3–8*

SEE PARALLEL PASSAGES AT MATTHEW 26:6–13 AND MARK 14:3–9

## 174. SEARCH FOR A YOUNG DONKEY

And when they [Jesus and His disciples] came near to Jerusalem, to Bethphage and Bethany, at the Mount of Olives, He sent forth two of His disciples and said to them, "Go your way into the village across from you, and as soon as you have entered into it, you shall find a colt tied, on which no man has ever sat. Untie it and bring it. And if any man says to you, 'Why are you doing this?' say that the Lord has need of it, and immediately he will send it here."

And they went their way and found the colt tied by the door outside in a place where two roads met, and they untied it. And some of those who stood there said to them, "What are you doing, untying the colt?" And they said to them just as Jesus had commanded, and they let them go.

And they brought the colt to Jesus and cast their garments on it, and He sat on it. *Mark 11:1–7*

## 175. THE TRIUMPHAL ENTRY INTO JERUSALEM

On the next day many people who had come to the feast, when they heard that Jesus was coming to Jerusalem, took branches of palm trees and went out to meet Him, and cried, "Hosanna! Blessed is the King of Israel who comes in the name of the Lord."

Crowds praise Jesus as He enters the Holy City on a donkey.

And Jesus, when He had found a young donkey, sat on it. As it is written, "Fear not, daughter of Zion; behold, your King comes, sitting on a donkey's colt." His disciples did not understand these things at the first, but when Jesus was glorified, then they remembered that these things were written of Him and that they had done these things to Him.

Therefore the people who were with Him when He called Lazarus out of his grave and raised him from the dead bore witness. For this reason the people also met Him, for they heard that He had done this miracle. Therefore the Pharisees said among themselves, "You perceive how you accomplish nothing? Behold, the world has gone after Him." *John 12:12–19*

See parallel accounts at Matthew 21:7–11;
Mark 11:8–11; and Luke 19:36–40

## 176. JESUS CURSES A FIG TREE AND DRIVES MERCHANTS FROM THE TEMPLE

And the next morning, when they [Jesus and His disciples] came from Bethany, He was hungry. And seeing a fig tree far off having leaves, He went to see if perhaps He might find anything on it. And when He came to it, He found nothing but leaves, for it was not yet the time of figs. And Jesus answered and said to it, "May no man eat fruit from you ever again." And His disciples heard it.

And they came to Jerusalem. And Jesus went into the temple, and began to cast out those who sold and bought in the temple, and overthrew the tables of the money changers and the seats of those who sold doves, and would not allow any man to carry any vessel through the temple.

And He taught, saying to them, "Is it not written, 'My house shall be called the house of prayer for all nations'? But you have made it a den of thieves."

And the scribes and chief priests heard it and were seeking how they might destroy Him. For they feared Him, because all the people were astonished at His doctrine. *Mark 11:12–18*

See parallel accounts at Matthew 21:12–19 and Luke 19:45–48

Jesus drives out merchants who have turned the temple into a "den of thieves."

Jesus received assurance,
from an audible voice from
heaven, that His death would
glorify God the Father.

And there were certain Greeks among them who came up to worship at the feast. Therefore the same came to Philip, who was of Bethsaida of Galilee, and asked him, saying, "Sir, we want to see Jesus." Philip came and told Andrew, and again Andrew and Philip told Jesus.

And Jesus answered them, saying, "The hour has come that the Son of Man should be glorified. Truly, truly, I say to you, unless a grain of wheat falls into the ground and dies, it remains alone. But if it dies, it brings forth much fruit. He who loves his life shall lose it, and he who hates his life in this world shall keep it to eternal life.

### "Father, Glorify Your Name"

"If any man serves Me, let him follow Me. And where I am, there My servant shall be also. If any man serves Me, My Father will honor him. Now My soul is troubled, and what shall I say? 'Father, save Me from this hour'? But for this reason I came to this hour. Father, glorify Your name."

Then there came a voice from heaven, saying, "I have both glorified it and will glorify it again." Therefore the people who stood by and heard it said that it thundered. Others said, "An angel spoke to Him."

Jesus answered and said, "This voice did not come because of Me, but for your sakes. Now is the judgment of this world. Now the prince of this world shall be cast out. And if I be lifted up from the earth, I will draw all men to Me." He said this signifying what death He would die.

The people answered Him, "We have heard from the Law that Christ remains forever. And how can You say, 'The Son of Man must be lifted up'? Who is this Son of Man?"

Then Jesus said to them, "The light is with you yet a little while. Walk while you have the light, lest darkness come on you, for he who walks in darkness does not know where he goes. While you have light, believe in the light, that you may be the children of light."

Jesus spoke these things and departed and hid Himself from them. *John 12:20–36*

## 178. GOD THE FATHER SPEAKS THROUGH JESUS

But though He [Jesus] had done so many miracles before them, they still did not believe in Him, that the saying of Isaiah the prophet might be fulfilled, which he spoke, "Lord, who has believed our report? And to whom has the arm of the Lord been revealed?"

Therefore they could not believe, because Isaiah said again, "He has blinded their eyes and hardened their hearts, that they should not see with their eyes or understand with their heart, and be converted, and I should heal them." Isaiah said these things when he saw His glory and spoke of Him.

Nevertheless many among the chief rulers also believed in Him, but because of the Pharisees they did not confess Him, lest they should be put out of the synagogue, for they loved the praise of men more than the praise of God.

## "I Have Come as a Light into the World"

Jesus cried and said, "He who believes in Me does not believe in Me but in Him who sent Me. And he who sees Me sees Him who sent Me. I have come as a light into the world, that whoever believes in Me should not abide in darkness. And if any man hears my words and does not believe, I do not judge him, for I came not to judge the world but to save the world.

"He who rejects Me and does not receive My words has one who judges him— the word that I have spoken. The same shall judge him in the last day. For I have not spoken of Myself, but the Father who sent me. He gave Me a commandment, what I should say and what I should speak. And I know that His commandment is everlasting life. Therefore whatever I speak, even as the Father said to Me, so I speak." *John 12:37–50*

# 179. MESSAGE FROM A DYING FIG TREE

And as they [Jesus and His disciples] passed by in the morning, they saw the fig tree dried up from the roots. And Peter, remembering, said to Him, "Master, look! The fig tree that You cursed has withered away."

Peter marvels at the withering fig tree that Jesus had cursed.

And answering, Jesus said to them, "Have faith in God. For truly I say to you that whoever shall say to this mountain, 'Be removed and be cast into the sea,' and shall not doubt in his heart but shall believe that those things that he says shall come to pass, he shall have whatever he says.

"Therefore I say to you, whatever things you desire when you pray, believe that you have received them, and you shall have them. And when you stand praying, forgive, if you have anything against anyone, that your Father who is in heaven may also forgive you for your trespasses." *Mark 11:20–25*

See parallel account at Matthew 21:19–22

## 180. JESUS' AUTHORITY QUESTIONED

And when He [Jesus] came into the temple, the chief priests and the elders of the people came to Him as He was teaching and said, "By what authority are You doing these things? And who gave You this authority?"

And Jesus answered and said to them, "I will also ask you one thing, which if you tell Me, I likewise will tell you by what authority I do these things: The baptism of John—from where did it come? From heaven or from men?"

And they reasoned among themselves, saying, "If we say, 'From heaven,' He will say to us, 'Why then did you not believe him?' But if we say, 'From men,' we fear the people, for all hold John as a prophet." And they answered Jesus and said, "We cannot tell."

And He said to them, "Neither will I tell you by what authority I do these things." *Matthew 21:23–27*

SEE PARALLEL ACCOUNTS AT MARK 11:27–33 AND LUKE 20:1–8

## 181. PARABLE OF TWO SONS AND A VINEYARD

[Jesus said]: "But what do you think? A certain man had two sons, and he came to the first and said, 'Son, go work today in my vineyard.'

"He answered and said, 'I will not,' but afterward he repented and went.

"And he came to the second and said likewise.

"And he answered and said, 'I will go, sir,' and did not go.

"Which of the two did the will of his father?"

They said to Him, "The first."

Jesus said to them, "Truly I say to you that the tax collectors and the harlots go into the kingdom of God before you. For John came to you in the way of righteousness, and you did not believe him. But the tax collectors and the harlots believed him. And you, when you saw it, did not repent afterward that you might believe him." *Matthew 21:28–32*

## 182. PARABLE OF THE EVIL VINEYARD WORKERS

[Jesus said]: "Hear another parable: There was a certain landowner who planted a vineyard and put a hedge around it, and dug a winepress in it, and built a tower, and leased it out to farmers and went into a far country.

"And when the time of the fruit drew near, he sent his servants to the farmers, that they might receive its fruits. And the farmers took his servants and beat one and killed another and stoned another. Again he sent other servants, more than the first, and they did likewise to them.

"But last of all he sent his son to them, saying, 'They will reverence my son.'

## A PARABLE WITH A TWIST

Jesus' parable about a murdered vineyard owner's son (see section 182) left no doubt that He was referring to the religious leaders of the Jewish nation who were determined to kill Him. Even they realized His words were directed at them. But ironically, they went right on plotting His death, fulfilling the violent intentions of the evil tenants whom Jesus described.

But when the farmers saw the son, they said among themselves, 'This is the heir. Come, let us kill him, and let us seize his inheritance.' And they caught him and cast him out of the vineyard and slew him.

"Therefore, when the lord of the vineyard comes, what will he do to those farmers?"

They said to Him, "He will miserably destroy those wicked men and will lease his vineyard to other farmers who shall render him the fruits in their seasons."

### "The Head of the Corner"

Jesus said to them, "Did you never read in the scriptures: 'The stone that the builders rejected, the same has become the head of the corner. This is the Lord's doing, and it is marvelous in our eyes'?

"Therefore I say to you, the kingdom of God shall be taken from you and given to a nation bringing forth its fruits. And whoever falls on this stone shall be broken. But on whomever it shall fall, it will grind him to powder."

And when the chief priests and Pharisees had heard His parables, they perceived that He was speaking of them. But when they sought to lay hands on Him, they feared the multitude, because they took Him for a prophet. *Matthew 21:33–46*

SEE PARALLEL ACCOUNTS AT MARK 12:1–12 AND LUKE 20:9–19

# 183. PARABLE OF A ROYAL WEDDING BANQUET

And Jesus answered and spoke to them [the religious leaders] again by parables and said: "The kingdom of heaven is similar to a certain king who made a marriage for his son and sent forth his servants to call those who were invited to the wedding. And they would not come.

"Again, he sent forth other servants, saying, 'Tell those who are invited, Behold, I have prepared my dinner. My oxen and my fattened cattle are killed, and all things are ready. Come to the marriage.'

"But they made light of it and went their ways, one to his farm, another to his business. And the rest took his servants, and treated them spitefully, and slew them. But when the king heard of it, he was angry. And he sent forth his armies and destroyed those murderers and burned up their city.

### "Those. . .Invited Were Not Worthy"

"Then he said to his servants, 'The wedding is ready, but those who were invited were not worthy. Therefore go into the highways and invite to the marriage as many as you find. So those servants went out into the highways and gathered together all, as many as they found, both bad and good. And the wedding was furnished with guests.

"And when the king came in to see the guests, he saw there a man who did not have on a wedding garment. And he said to him, 'Friend, how did you come in here not having a wedding garment?' And he was speechless.

"Then the king said to the servants, 'Bind him hand and foot, and take him away, and cast him into outer darkness. There shall be weeping and gnashing of teeth.' For many are called, but few are chosen." *Matthew 22:1–14*

Jesus' first miracle occurred at a wedding. Much later, He delivered a parable about a wedding feast to Jewish religious leaders.

## 184. A TRICK QUESTION ABOUT TAXES

Then the Pharisees went and took counsel how they might entangle Him [Jesus] in His talk. And they sent out their disciples to Him, with the Herodians, saying, "Master, we know that You are true and teach the way of God in truth. You do not care for any man, for You do not regard the person of men. Tell us, therefore, what do You think? Is it lawful to give tax to Caesar or not?"

But Jesus perceived their wickedness and said, "Why do you tempt Me, you hypocrites? Show Me the tax money." And they brought to Him a penny.

And He said to them, "Whose is this image and inscription?"

They said to Him, "Caesar's."

Then He said to them, "Therefore render to Caesar the things that are Caesar's and to God the things that are God's." When they had heard these words, they marveled and left Him and went their way. *Matthew 22:15–22*

SEE PARALLEL ACCOUNTS AT MARK 12:13–17 AND LUKE 20:20–26

A Pharisee asks Jesus about paying taxes to the Roman government.

## 185. MARRIAGE AND THE AFTERLIFE

Then some of the Sadducees, who deny that there is any resurrection, came to Him [Jesus], and they asked Him, saying, "Master, Moses wrote for us that if any man's brother dies, having a wife, and he dies without children, that his brother should take his wife and raise up children for his brother.

"Therefore there were seven brothers. And the first took a wife and died without children. And the second took her as wife, and he died childless. And the third took her, and in like manner the seven also. And they left no children and died.

Last of all the woman also died. Therefore, in the resurrection, whose wife is she? For seven had her as a wife."

### "Children of the Resurrection"

And Jesus answered and said to them, "The children of this world marry and are given in marriage. But those who shall be accounted worthy to obtain that world, and the resurrection from the dead, neither marry nor are given in marriage. Nor can they die anymore, for they are equal to the angels and are the children of God, being the children of the resurrection.

"Now even Moses showed at the bush that the dead are raised when he called the Lord 'the God of Abraham, and the God of Isaac, and the God of Jacob.' For He is not a God of the dead but of the living, for all live to Him."

Then some of the scribes answered and said, "Master, You have said well." And after that they dared not ask Him any question at all. *Luke 20:27–40*

SEE PARALLEL ACCOUNTS AT MATTHEW 22:23–33 AND MARK 12:18–27

## 186. THE GREATEST COMMANDMENT

And one of the scribes came, and having heard them reasoning together, and perceiving that He [Jesus] had answered them well, asked Him, "Which commandment is the first of all?"

And Jesus answered him, "The first of all the commandments is 'Hear, O Israel: The Lord our God is one Lord. And you shall love the Lord your God with all your heart and with all your soul and with all your mind and with all your strength.' This is the first commandment. And the second—namely this—is similar: 'You shall love your neighbor as yourself.' There is no other commandment greater than these."

And the scribe said to Him, "Well said, Master. You have said the truth, for there is one God, and there is no other but Him. And to love Him with all the heart and with all the understanding and with all the soul and with all the strength, and to love one's neighbor as oneself, is more than all the whole burnt offerings and sacrifices."

And when Jesus saw that he answered discreetly, He said to him, "You are not far from the kingdom of God." And after that no man dared ask Him any questions. *Mark 12:28–34*

SEE PARALLEL ACCOUNT AT MATTHEW 22:34–40

## 187. HYPOCRISY OF THE SCRIBES AND PHARISEES

Then Jesus spoke to the multitude and to His disciples, saying, "The scribes and the Pharisees sit in Moses' seat. Therefore whatever they tell you to observe, observe and do that. But do not do according to their works. For they say, and do not do.

"For they bind heavy burdens, and grievous to be borne, and lay them on men's shoulders. But they themselves will not move them with one of their fingers. But

A modern Jewish man puts on a phylactery—a small box containing a verse of scripture. Jesus criticized the Jews of His day for emphasizing such externals.

they do all their works to be seen by men.

"They make their phylacteries broad and enlarge the borders of their garments, and love the best places at feasts, and the chief seats in the synagogues, and greetings in the markets, and to be called by men, 'Rabbi, Rabbi.'" *Matthew 23:1–7*

## 188. WOEFUL ACTIONS OF THE SCRIBES AND PHARISEES

[Jesus said]: "But woe to you, scribes and Pharisees, hypocrites! For you shut up the kingdom of heaven against men. For you neither go in yourselves, nor do you allow those who are entering to go in.

"Woe to you, scribes and Pharisees, hypocrites! For you devour widows' houses, and for a false show make long prayers. Therefore you shall receive the greater damnation.

"Woe to you, scribes and Pharisees, hypocrites! For you travel around sea and land to make one proselyte, and when he is made, you make him twofold more the child of hell than yourselves.

### "Blind Guides"

"Woe to you, you blind guides, who say, 'Whoever swears by the temple, it is nothing. But whoever swears by the gold of the temple, he is a debtor!' You blind fools! For which is greater, the gold or the temple that sanctifies the gold? And,

'Whoever swears by the altar, it is nothing. But whoever swears by the gift that is on it, he is guilty.' You blind fools! For which is greater, the gift or the altar that sanctifies the gift?

"Therefore whoever swears by the altar, swears by it and by all things on it. And whoever swears by the temple, swears by it and by Him who dwells in it. And he who swears by heaven, swears by the throne of God and by Him who sits on it.

"Woe to you, scribes and Pharisees, hypocrites! For you pay tithe of mint and anise and cumin, and have omitted the weightier matters of the law: judgment, mercy, and faith. These you ought to have done, and not leave the others undone. You blind guides, who strain out a gnat and swallow a camel.

"Woe to you, scribes and Pharisees, hypocrites! For you make the outside of the cup and of the platter clean, but inside they are full of extortion and excess. You blind Pharisee! First clean what is inside the cup and platter, that the outside of them may be clean also.

### "Whitewashed Sepulchres"

"Woe to you, scribes and Pharisees, hypocrites! For you are similar to whitewashed sepulchres that indeed appear beautiful outwardly, but inside are full of dead men's bones and of all uncleanness. Even so you also outwardly appear righteous to men, but inside you are full of hypocrisy and iniquity.

"Woe to you, scribes and Pharisees, hypocrites! Because you build the tombs of the prophets and garnish the sepulchres of the righteous, and say, 'If we had been in the days of our fathers, we would not have been partakers with them in the blood of the prophets.'

"Therefore you are witnesses to yourselves that you are the children of those who killed the prophets. Fill up, then, the measure of your fathers. You serpents, you generation of vipers, how can you escape the damnation of hell?

"Therefore, behold, I send to you prophets, and wise men, and scribes. And some of them you shall kill and crucify, and some of them you shall scourge in your synagogues and persecute from city to city, that on you may come all the righteous blood shed on the earth, from the blood of righteous Abel to the blood of Zechariah, son of Berechiah, whom you slew between the temple and the altar. Truly I say to you, all these things shall come on this generation." *Matthew 23:13–36*

SEE PARALLEL ACCOUNTS AT MARK 12:38–40 AND LUKE 20:45–47

## WOE AFTER WOE AFTER WOE

Matthew 23 is known as the "woe chapter" of the Gospels because of its series of woes that Jesus pronounced against the scribes and Pharisees (see sections 187 and 188). He charged them with trying to impress people by making a public display of their religiosity, keeping people from entering the kingdom of God with their misleading teachings, seeking public recognition, rejecting the prophets sent by the Lord, and majoring on minor issues such as ritualism while ignoring more important matters such as mercy and justice.

And Jesus sat across from the treasury and saw how the people cast money into the treasury. And many who were rich cast in much. And a certain poor widow came, and she threw in two mites, which make a farthing.

And He called His disciples to Himself and said to them, "Truly I say to you that this poor widow has cast in more than all those who have cast into the treasury, for all those cast in out of their abundance, but she, out of her need, cast in all that she had, even all her living." *Mark 12:41–44*

SEE PARALLEL ACCOUNT AT LUKE 21:1–4

Jesus commends the meager offering of a poor widow.

## 190. JESUS PREDICTS THE DESTRUCTION OF JERUSALEM

And Jesus went out and departed from the temple, and His disciples came to Him to show Him the buildings of the temple. And Jesus said to them, "Do you not see all these things? Truly I say to you, there shall not be one stone left here on another, that shall not be thrown down."

And as He sat upon the Mount of Olives, the disciples came to Him privately, saying, "Tell us, when shall these things be? And what shall be the sign of Your coming, and of the end of the world?"

And Jesus answered and said to them, "Be careful that no man deceives you. For many shall come in My name, saying, 'I am Christ,' and shall deceive many. And you shall hear of wars and rumors of wars. See that you are not troubled. For all these things must come to pass, but the end is not yet.

### "Beginning of Sorrows"

"For nation shall rise against nation, and kingdom against kingdom. And there shall be famines and pestilences and earthquakes in various places. All these are the beginning of sorrows.

"Then they shall deliver you up to be afflicted and shall kill you, and you shall be hated by all nations for My name's sake. And then many shall fall away, and shall betray one another, and shall hate one another. And many false prophets shall rise and shall deceive many.

"And because iniquity shall abound, the love of many shall grow cold. But he who endures to the end, the same shall be saved. And this gospel of the kingdom shall be preached in all the world as a witness to all nations, and then the end shall come." *Matthew 24:1–14*

SEE PARALLEL ACCOUNTS AT MARK 13:1–13 AND LUKE 21:5–19

## 191. TERRIFYING EVENTS OF THIS PERILOUS TIME

[Jesus said]: "Therefore when you see the abomination of desolation, spoken of by Daniel the prophet, stand in the holy place (whoever reads, let him understand), then let those who are in Judea flee into the mountains. Let him who is on the housetop not come down to take anything out of his house.

"Do not let him who is in the field return back to take his clothes. And woe to those who are with child and to those who nurse children in those days! But pray that your flight is not in the winter or on the Sabbath day. For then there shall be great tribulation, such as has not been since the beginning of the world to this time, no, nor ever shall be. And unless those days were shortened, no flesh would be saved. But for the elect's sake those days shall be shortened.

197

"Then if any man says to you, 'Look, here is Christ,' or 'There,' do not believe it. For false christs and false prophets shall arise and shall show great signs and wonders, to such a degree that, if it were possible, they shall deceive the very elect. Behold, I have told you before." *Matthew 24:15–25*

SEE PARALLEL ACCOUNTS AT MARK 13:14–23 AND LUKE 21:20–24

On a hill overlooking Jerusalem, Jesus predicts the destruction of the city as well as awesome events that will occur at the end of the age.

## 192. THE END OF THE AGE AND JESUS' SECOND COMING

[Jesus said]: "Therefore if they say to you, 'Behold, He [the Son of Man] is in the desert,' do not go forth; or 'Behold, He is in the secret chambers,' do not believe it. For as the lightning comes out of the east and shines even to the west, so also shall be the coming of the Son of Man. For wherever the carcass is, there the eagles will be gathered together.

"Immediately after the tribulation of those days the sun shall be darkened, and the moon shall not give its light, and the stars shall fall from heaven, and the powers of the heavens shall be shaken.

"And then the sign of the Son of Man shall appear in heaven, and then all the tribes of the earth shall mourn, and they shall see the Son of Man coming in the clouds of heaven with power and great glory. And He shall send His angels with a great sound of a trumpet, and they shall gather together His elect from the four winds, from one end of heaven to the other."

"Now learn a parable from the fig tree: When its branch is yet tender and puts forth leaves, you know that summer is near. So you, likewise, when you see all these things, know that it is near—even at the doors. Truly I say to you, this generation shall not pass till all these things are fulfilled. Heaven and earth shall pass away, but My words shall not pass away." *Matthew 24:26–35*

SEE PARALLEL ACCOUNTS AT MARK 13:24–31 AND LUKE 21:25–33

## 193. UNCERTAIN TIME OF JESUS' RETURN

[Jesus said]: "But as the days of Noah were, so also shall be the coming of the Son of Man. For as in the days that were before the flood, they were eating and drinking, marrying and giving in marriage, until the day that Noah entered into the ark, and did not know until the flood came and took them all away, so also shall be the coming of the Son of Man.

"Then two shall be in the field; the one shall be taken and the other left. Two women shall be grinding at the mill; the one shall be taken and the other left. Watch, therefore, for you do not know what hour your Lord will come.

"But know this, that if the master of the house had known in what watch the thief would come, he would have watched and would not have allowed his house to be broken into. Therefore you also be ready, for the Son of Man is coming at such an hour as you do not think.

"Who then is a faithful and wise servant, whom his lord has made ruler over his household, to give them food in due season? Blessed is that servant whom his lord, when he comes, shall find so doing. Truly, I say to you that he shall make him ruler over all his goods.

Jesus declared that angels and trumpet sounds will announce His return.

"But if that evil servant says in his heart, 'My lord delays his coming,' and begins to strike his fellow servants, and to eat and drink with the drunken, then the lord of that servant shall come in a day when he does not look for him and in an hour that he is not aware of, and shall cut him in pieces and appoint him his portion with the hypocrites. There shall be weeping and gnashing of teeth." *Matthew 24:37–51*

SEE PARALLEL ACCOUNTS AT MARK 13:33–37 AND LUKE 21:34–36

## 194. PARABLE OF THE TEN VIRGINS

[Jesus said]: "Then the kingdom of heaven shall be compared to ten virgins who took their lamps and went forth to meet the bridegroom. And five of them were wise, and five were foolish. Those who were foolish took their lamps and took no oil with them, but the wise took oil in their vessels with their lamps. While the bridegroom delayed, they all slumbered and slept.

"And at midnight there was a cry made: 'Behold, the bridegroom is coming. Go out to meet him.' Then all those virgins arose and trimmed their lamps. And the foolish said to the wise, 'Give us some of your oil, for our lamps are going out.'

"But the wise answered, saying, 'No, lest there be not enough for us and you. But go rather to those who sell, and buy for yourselves.' And while they went to buy, the bridegroom came, and those who were ready went in with him to the marriage, and the door was shut. Afterward the other virgins also came, saying, 'Lord, Lord, open to us.' But he answered and said, 'Truly I say to you, I do not know you.'

"Watch therefore, for you know neither the day nor the hour in which the Son of Man is coming." *Matthew 25:1–13*

## 195. PARABLE OF THE TALENTS

[Jesus said]: "For the kingdom of heaven is as a man traveling into a far country, who called his own servants and delivered to them his goods. And to one he gave five talents, to another two, and to another one, to every man according to his separate ability, and immediately took his journey.

"Then he who had received the five talents went and traded with the same, and made them another five talents. And likewise he who had received two, he gained two others also. But he who had received one went and dug in the earth and hid his lord's money. After a long time the lord of those servants came and settled accounts with them.

### "Well Done. . .Faithful Servant"

"And so he who had received five talents came and brought another five talents, saying, 'Lord, you delivered to me five talents. Behold, I have gained five more talents besides them.'

"His lord said to him, 'Well done, good and faithful servant. You have been

In Jesus' parable, a servant is
rewarded for his shrewd management
of his master's resources.

faithful over a few things; I will make you ruler over many things. Enter into the joy of your lord.'

"He who had received two talents also came and said, 'Lord, you delivered to me two talents. Behold, I have gained two other talents besides them.'

"His lord said to him, 'Well done, good and faithful servant. You have been faithful over a few things; I will make you ruler over many things. Enter into the joy of your lord.'

## "You Wicked and Slothful Servant"

"Then he who had received the one talent came and said, 'Lord, I knew you, that you are a hard man, reaping where you have not sown and gathering where you have not scattered. And I was afraid and went and hid your talent in the earth. Look, there you have what is yours.'

"His lord answered and said to him, 'You wicked and slothful servant. You knew that I reap where I did not sow and gather where I have not scattered. Therefore you ought to have put my money to the exchangers, and then at my coming I should have received my own with interest. Therefore take the talent from him, and give it to him who has ten talents.'

"For to everyone who has, more shall be given, and he shall have abundance. But from him who does not have, even what he has shall be taken away. And cast the unprofitable servant into outer darkness. There shall be weeping and gnashing of teeth." *Matthew 25:14–30*

# 196. PARABLE OF THE SHEEP AND GOATS

[Jesus said]: "When the Son of Man comes in His glory, and all the holy angels with Him, then He shall sit on the throne of His glory. And all nations shall be gathered before Him, and He shall separate them one from another, as a shepherd divides his sheep from the goats. And He shall set the sheep on His right hand, but the goats on the left.

"Then the King shall say to those on His right hand, 'Come, you blessed of My Father, inherit the kingdom prepared for you from the foundation of the world. For I was hungry and you gave Me food; I was thirsty and you gave Me drink; I was a stranger and you took Me in; naked and you clothed Me; I was sick and you visited Me; I was in prison and you came to Me.'

"Then the righteous shall answer Him, saying, 'Lord, when did we see You hungry and feed You? Or thirsty and give You drink? When did we see You a stranger and take You in? Or naked and clothe You? Or when did we see You sick, or in prison, and come to You?'

"And the King shall answer and say to them, 'Truly I say to you, because you have done it to one of the least of these My brothers, you have done it to Me.'

Sheep and goats grazing together recall Jesus' parable about the great separation of people at the end of the age.

## "Depart from Me"

"Then He shall also say to those on the left hand, 'Depart from Me, you cursed, into everlasting fire prepared for the devil and his angels. For I was hungry and you gave Me no food; I was thirsty and you gave Me no drink; I was a stranger and you did not take Me in; naked and you did not clothe me; sick and in prison and you did not visit Me.'

"Then they also shall answer Him, saying, 'Lord, when did we see You hungry or thirsty or a stranger or naked or sick or in prison, and did not minister to You?'

"Then He shall answer them, saying, 'Truly I say to you, because you did not do it to one of the least of these, you did not do it to Me.' And these shall go away into everlasting punishment, but the righteous into eternal life." *Matthew 25:31–46*

## 197. JUDAS MAKES A DEAL

Then one of the twelve, called Judas Iscariot, went to the chief priests and said to them, "What will you give me, and I will deliver Him [Jesus] to you?" And they covenanted with him for thirty pieces of silver. And from that time he sought opportunity to betray Him. *Matthew 26:14–16*

SEE PARALLEL ACCOUNTS AT MARK 14:10–11 AND LUKE 22:3–6

Judas receives the "blood money" he was paid to betray Jesus.

## 198. PREPARATIONS FOR THE PASSOVER MEAL

Then came the day of Unleavened Bread, when the Passover must be killed. And He [Jesus] sent Peter and John, saying, "Go and prepare the Passover for us, that we may eat."

And they said to Him, "Where do You want us to prepare?"

And He said to them, "Behold, when you have entered into the city, a man bearing a pitcher of water shall meet you. Follow him into the house where he enters. And you shall say to the master of the house, 'The Master says to you, "Where is the guest chamber, where I shall eat the Passover with My disciples?"' And he shall show you a large, furnished upper room. Prepare it there."

And they went and found it as He had said to them, and they prepared the Passover. *Luke 22:7–13*

SEE PARALLEL PASSAGES AT MATTHEW 26:17–19 AND MARK 14:12–16

## 199. WHICH DISCIPLE IS THE GREATEST?

And when the hour had come [for the Passover meal], He [Jesus] sat down, and the twelve apostles with Him. And He said to them, "With desire I have desired to eat this Passover with you before I suffer. For I say to you, I will not eat of it anymore until it is fulfilled in the kingdom of God." *Luke 22:14–16*

And there was also a strife among them [Jesus' disciples], as to which of them should be considered the greatest. And He said to them, "The kings of the Gentiles exercise lordship over them, and those who exercise authority over them are called benefactors.

"But you shall not be so. But he who is greatest among you, let him be as the younger, and he who is chief, as he who serves. For who is greater, he who sits at the table or he who serves? Is it not he who sits at the table? But I am among you as He who serves." *Luke 22:24–27*

At the last supper, Jesus reminded His squabbling disciples that service to others is the mark of true greatness.

## 200. AN OBJECT LESSON IN HUMBLE SERVICE

Jesus, knowing that the Father had given all things into His hands, and that He had come from God and went to God, He rose from supper and laid aside His garments and took a towel and girded Himself. After that, He poured water into a basin and began to wash the disciples' feet, and to wipe them with the towel with which He was girded.

Then He came to Simon Peter. And Peter said to Him, "Lord, do You wash my feet?"

Jesus sets an example of humble service by washing His disciples' feet.

Jesus answered and said to him, "What I do you do not understand now, but you shall understand hereafter."

Peter said to Him, "You shall never wash my feet."

Jesus answered him, "If I do not wash you, you have no part with Me."

Simon Peter said to Him, "Lord, not only my feet, but also my hands and my head."

Jesus said to him, "He who is washed needs only to wash his feet, but is every bit clean. And you are clean, but not all." For He knew who would betray Him; therefore He said, "You are not all clean."

### "You. . .Wash One Another's Feet"

So after He had washed their feet, and had taken His garments, and had sat down again, He said to them, "Do you know what I have done to you? You call Me Master and Lord, and you are right to say it, for so I am. If I then, your Lord and Master, have washed your feet, you also ought to wash one another's feet. For I have given you an example, that you should do as I have done to you.

"Truly, truly, I say to you, the servant is not greater than his master, nor is he who is sent greater than he who sent him. If you understand these things, you are happy if you do them." *John 13:3–17*

## 201. JUDAS IDENTIFIED AS THE BETRAYER

When Jesus had said this, He was troubled in spirit and testified and said, "Truly, truly, I say to you that one of you shall betray Me."

Then the disciples looked at one another, doubting of whom He spoke. Now there was one of His disciples, whom Jesus loved, leaning on Jesus' chest. Therefore Simon Peter beckoned to him, that he should ask who it should be of whom He spoke. Then, lying on Jesus' chest, he said to Him, "Lord, who is it?"

Jesus answered, "It is he to whom I shall give a piece of bread when I have dipped it." And when He had dipped the piece of bread, He gave it to Judas Iscariot, the son of Simon. And after the piece of bread, Satan entered into him.

Then Jesus said to him, "What you do, do quickly." Now no man at the table knew why He spoke this to him. For some of them thought, because Judas had the bag, that Jesus had said to him, "Buy those things that we have need of in preparation for the feast," or that he should give something to the poor. Having received the piece of bread, he then went out immediately. And it was night. *John 13:21–30*

SEE PARALLEL ACCOUNTS AT MATTHEW 26:21–25;
MARK 14:18–21; AND LUKE 22:21–23

## 202. A NEW COMMANDMENT FOR THE TWELVE

Therefore, when he [Judas] had gone out, Jesus said, "Now is the Son of Man glorified, and God is glorified in Him. If God is glorified in Him, God shall also glorify Him in Himself, and shall glorify Him immediately.

"Little children, I am with you yet a little while. You shall seek Me, and as I said to the Jews, 'Where I go, you cannot come,' so now I say to you. A new commandment I give to you, that you love one another; as I have loved you, that you also love one another. By this shall all men know that you are My disciples, if you have love for one another." *John 13:31–35*

## 203. PREDICTION OF THE DISCIPLES' DENIAL

Then Jesus said to them [His disciples], "All of you shall be made to stumble because of Me this night, for it is written: 'I will strike the shepherd, and the sheep of the flock shall be scattered abroad.' But after I have risen again, I will go before you into Galilee."

Peter answered and said to Him, "Though all men shall be made to stumble because of You, yet I will never be made to stumble."

Jesus said to him, "Truly I say to you that this night, before the rooster crows, you shall deny Me three times."

Peter said to Him, "Though I should die with You, still I will not deny You." All the disciples also said likewise. *Matthew 26:31–35*

SEE PARALLEL ACCOUNTS AT MARK 14:27–31;
LUKE 22:31–34; AND JOHN 13:37–38

## 204. A MEMORIAL OF JESUS' DEATH

And when the hour had come, He [Jesus] sat down, and the twelve apostles with Him. And He said to them, "With desire I have desired to eat this Passover with you before I suffer. For I say to you, I will not eat of it anymore until it is fulfilled in the kingdom of God."

And He took the cup, and gave thanks, and said, "Take this and divide it among yourselves. For I say to you, I will not drink of the fruit of the vine until the kingdom of God comes."

And He took bread, and gave thanks and broke it, and gave to them, saying, "This is My body that is given for you. Do this in remembrance of Me."

Likewise He also took the cup after supper, saying, "This cup is the new covenant in My blood, which is shed for you." *Luke 22:14–20*

SEE PARALLEL ACCOUNTS
AT MATTHEW 26:26–29
AND MARK 14:22–25

Jesus turned the Passover meal with His disciples into a ritual of remembrance of His sacrificial death.

## A SPECIAL MEAL

The meal that Jesus and His disciples ate together (see section 204) was part of a Jewish festival known as Passover. It commemorated the Exodus from Egypt many centuries before when the Lord "passed over" Israelite households while striking the firstborn children of Egyptian families (Exodus 12:26–29). Jesus turned this Jewish tradition into a memorial of His approaching death. It is observed today by different Christian groups as the Lord's Supper, Holy Communion, Eucharist, or Mass.

A few days after this memorial meal, Jesus was crucified in Jerusalem while the Passover celebration was going on. Early Christians saw the connection between His sacrificial death and that of a lamb which was traditionally eaten during this holiday. The apostle Paul referred to Jesus as "our Passover. . . sacrificed for us" (1 Corinthians 5:7).

## 205. A FOND FAREWELL TO THE TWELVE

[Jesus said to His disciples]: "Do not let your hearts be troubled; you believe in God, believe also in Me. In my Father's house are many mansions; if it were not so, I would have told you. I go to prepare a place for you. And if I go and prepare a place for you, I will come again and receive you to Myself, that where I am, there you may be also. And you know where I go, and you know the way."

Thomas said to Him, "Lord, we do not know where You go, and how can we know the way?"

Jesus said to him, "I am the way, the truth, and the life. No man comes to the Father except through Me." If you had known Me, you would have known my Father also. And from now on you know Him and have seen Him."

### "I Am in the Father"

Philip said to Him, "Lord, show us the Father, and it is sufficient for us."

Jesus said to him, "Have I been with you so long, and still you have not known Me, Philip? He who has seen Me has seen the Father. And how do you say then, 'Show us the Father'? Do you not believe that I am in the Father and the Father in Me? The words that I speak to you I speak not of Myself, but the Father who dwells in Me, He does the works. Believe Me that I am in the Father and the Father in Me, or else believe Me for the very works' sake.

"Truly, truly, I say to you, he who believes in Me, the works that I do he shall do also. And greater works than these he shall do, because I go to My Father. And whatever you ask in My name, that I will do, that the Father may be glorified in the Son. If you ask anything in My name, I will do it.

"If you love Me, keep My commandments." *John 14:1–15*

## 206. THE COMING COMFORTER

[Jesus said to His disciples]: And I will pray to the Father, and He shall give you another Comforter, that He may abide with you forever—even the Spirit of truth, whom the world cannot receive, because it does not see Him, nor does it know Him. But you know Him, for He dwells with you and shall be in you. I will not leave you comfortless; I will come to you.

"Yet a little while, and the world will see Me no more, but you see Me. Because I live, you shall live also. On that day you shall know that I am in My Father, and you in Me, and I in you. He who has My commandments and keeps them, it is he who loves Me. And he who loves Me shall be loved by My Father, and I will love him, and will reveal Myself to him."

Judas (not Iscariot) said to Him, "Lord, how is it that You will reveal Yourself to us and not to the world?"

Jesus answered and said to him, "If a man loves Me, he will keep My words, and My Father will love him, and We will come to him and make Our dwelling with him. He who does not love Me does not keep My sayings, and the word that you hear is not Mine but the Father's who sent Me.

### "The Comforter. . .Shall Teach You All Things"

"These things I have spoken to you, being yet present with you. But the Comforter, who is the Holy Spirit, whom the Father will send in My name, He shall teach you all things and bring to your remembrance all things that I have said to you.

"I leave peace with you; I give to you My peace. I do not give to you as the world gives. Do not let your heart be troubled or let it be afraid. You have heard how I said to you, 'I go away and come again to you.' If you loved Me, you would rejoice because I said, 'I go to the Father,' for My Father is greater than I.

"And now I have told you before it comes to pass, that when it has come to pass, you might believe. From now on I will not talk much with you, for the prince of this world comes, and has nothing in Me. But that the world may know that I love the Father, and as the Father gave Me commandment, even so I do.

"Arise, let us go from here." *John 14:16–31*

## 207. JESUS AS THE TRUE VINE

[Jesus said to His disciples]: "I am the true vine, and My Father is the vinedresser. Every branch in Me that does not bear fruit He takes away, and every branch that bears fruit He purges, that it may bring forth more fruit. Now you are clean through the word that I have spoken to you. Abide in Me, and I in you. As the branch cannot bear fruit by itself, unless it abides in the vine, no more can you, unless you abide in Me.

"I am the vine; you are the branches. He who abides in Me, and I in him, the same brings forth much fruit. For without Me you can do nothing. If a man does not abide in Me, he is cast forth as a branch and is withered, and men gather them and cast them into the fire, and they are burned. If you abide in Me, and My words abide in you, you shall ask what you will, and it shall be done for you. In this My Father is glorified, that you bear much fruit; so you shall be My disciples.

## STRENGTH FOR THE FUTURE

Jesus encouraged His disciples during the Last Supper to remain attached to Him as the true vine (see section 207). This imagery came from a grapevine, a familiar domestic crop during Bible times.

A grapevine has one main stem with numerous smaller shoots branching off in all directions. These runners draw their sustenance from the main trunk. In the same way, Jesus was saying, the disciples should depend on Him for strength to serve as His witnesses after His resurrection and ascension to God the Father.

"As the Father has loved Me, so have I loved you; continue in My love. If you keep My commandments, you shall abide in My love, even as I have kept My Father's commandments and abide in His love. These things I have spoken to you, that My joy might remain in you, and that your joy might be full." *John 15:1–11*

## 208. THE CONTINUING WITNESS OF THE TWELVE

[Jesus said to His disciples]: "If the world hates you, you know that it hated Me before it hated you. If you were of the world, the world would love its own. But because you are not of the world, but I have chosen you out of the world, therefore the world hates you.

"Remember the word that I said to you, 'The servant is not greater than his master.' If they have persecuted Me, they will also persecute you. If they have kept My saying, they will keep yours also. But they will do all these things to you for My name's sake, because they do not know Him who sent Me. If I had not come and spoken to them, they would not have had sin, but now they have no excuse for their sin.

"He who hates me also hates My Father. If I had not done among them the works that no other man did, they would not have had sin, but now they have both seen and hated both Me and My Father. But this comes to pass that the word might be fulfilled that is written in their Law: 'They hated Me without a cause.'

"But when the Comforter comes, whom I will send to you from the Father, even the Spirit of truth who proceeds from the Father, He shall testify of Me. And you shall also bear witness, because you have been with Me from the beginning." *John 15:18–27*

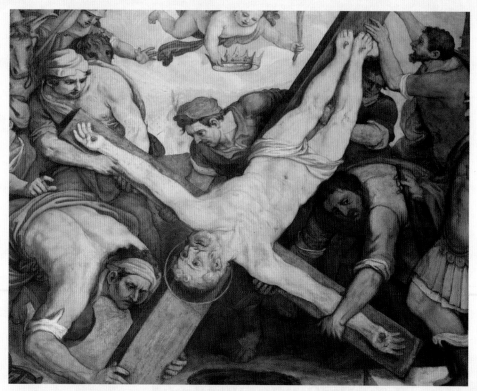

Legend says that Peter, like Jesus, was crucified—but he asked to be hung upside down since he didn't feel worthy of dying as Jesus had. The Lord had promised His disciples that they would encounter opposition and persecution.

## 209. JESUS' VICTORY OVER THE WORLD

[Jesus said to His disciples]: "I have spoken these things to you in proverbs, but the time is coming when I shall speak to you no longer in proverbs, but I shall tell you plainly about the Father. On that day you shall ask in My name, and I do not say to you that I will ask the Father for you.

"For the Father Himself loves you because you have loved Me and have believed that I came from God. I came forth from the Father and have come into the world. Again, I leave the world and go to the Father."

His disciples said to Him, "Behold, now You speak plainly and do not speak a proverb. Now we are sure that You know all things and do not need any man to ask You. By this we believe that You came forth from God."

Jesus answered them, "Do you now believe? Behold, the hour is coming, yes, has now come, that you shall be scattered, every man to his own, and shall leave Me alone. And yet I am not alone because the Father is with Me. I have spoken these things to you, that in Me you might have peace. In the world you shall have tribulation, but be of good cheer: I have overcome the world." *John 16:25–33*

## 210. JESUS PRAYS THAT HIS DEATH WILL GLORIFY GOD

Jesus spoke these words, and lifted up His eyes to heaven, and said, "Father, the hour has come. Glorify Your Son, that Your Son may also glorify You, as You have given Him power over all flesh, that He should give eternal life to as many as You have given Him. And this is life eternal, that they might know You, the only true God, and Jesus Christ whom You have sent.

"I have glorified You on the earth. I have finished the work that You gave Me to do. And now, O Father, glorify Me with Yourself, with the glory that I had with You before the world was."
*John 17:1–5*

Jesus declared in prayer that He had finished the work that God the Father sent Him to do.

## 211. JESUS PRAYS FOR HIS DISCIPLES

[Jesus prayed]: "I have made Your name known to the men whom You gave Me out of the world. They were Yours, and You gave them to Me, and they have kept Your word. Now they have known that all things that You have given Me are from You. For I have given to them the words that You gave Me, and they have received them and have surely known that I came from You. And they have believed that You sent Me.

"I pray for them. I do not pray for the world, but for those whom You have given Me, for they are Yours. And all Mine are Yours, and Yours are Mine, and I am glorified in them. And now I am no longer in the world, but they are in the world, and I am coming to You.

### A THREE-FOLD PRAYER

Jesus' words in John 17 (see sections 210–212) form His longest recorded prayer in the Gospels. It is called His "high priestly prayer" because He took on the role of Israel's high priest in praying for Himself, His disciples, and all future believers.

In this passionate prayer, Jesus looked beyond His approaching death. He expressed confidence that His sacrifice would be an undeniable expression of God's love for all people of the world.

### "That They May Be One"

"Holy Father, keep through Your own name those whom You have given Me, that they may be one, as We are. While I was with them in the world, I kept them in Your name. I have kept those whom You gave Me, and none of them is lost but the son of perdition, that the scripture might be fulfilled.

"And now I come to You, and these things I speak in the world, that they might have My joy fulfilled in themselves. I have given them Your word, and the world has hated them because they are not of the world, even as I am not of the world. I do not ask that You take them out of the world, but that You would keep them from evil. They are not of the world, even as I am not of the world.

"Sanctify them through Your truth. Your word is truth. As You have sent Me into the world, even so I have also sent them into the world. And for their sakes I sanctify Myself, that they also might be sanctified through the truth." *John 17:6–19*

## 212. JESUS PRAYS FOR ALL FUTURE BELIEVERS

[Jesus prayed]: "I do not ask for these [His disciples] alone, but also for those who shall believe in Me through their word, that they all may be one, as You, Father, are in Me, and I in You, that they also may be one in Us, that the world may believe that You have sent Me.

"And I have given them the glory that You gave Me, that they may be one, even as We are one: I in them, and You in Me, that they may be made perfect in unity and that the world may know that You have sent Me and have loved them as You have loved Me.

"Father, I desire that they, whom You have given Me, may also be with Me where I am, that they may behold My glory, which You have given Me. For You loved Me before the foundation of the world.

"O righteous Father, the world has not known You, but I have known You, and these have known that You have sent Me. And I have declared Your name to them and will declare it, that the love with which You have loved Me may be in them, and I in them." *John 17:20–26*

## 213. A DARK HOUR IN GETHSEMANE

And when they [Jesus and His disciples] had sung a hymn, they went out to the Mount of Olives. *Matthew 26:30*

Then Jesus came with them to a place called Gethsemane and said to the disciples, "Sit here while I go and pray over there." And He took with Him Peter and the two sons of Zebedee, and began to be sorrowful and very heavy. Then He said to them, "My soul is exceedingly sorrowful, even to death. Remain here and watch with Me."

Struggling over His approaching death, Jesus prays to His Father, "Your will be done."

And He went a little farther and fell on His face, and prayed, saying, "O My Father, if it is possible, let this cup pass from Me. Nevertheless, not as I will, but as You will."

And He came to the disciples and found them asleep, and said to Peter, "What, could you not watch with Me one hour? Watch and pray, that you do not enter into temptation. The spirit indeed is willing, but the flesh is weak."

## "Your Will Be Done"

He went away again the second time and prayed, saying, "O My Father, if this cup may not pass away from Me unless I drink it, Your will be done." And He came and found them asleep again, for their eyes were heavy.

And He left them and went away again, and prayed the third time, saying the same words. Then He came to His disciples and said to them, "Sleep on now, and take your rest. Behold, the hour is at hand, and the Son of Man is being betrayed into the hands of sinners. Rise, let us be going. Behold, he who betrays Me is at hand." *Matthew 26:36–46*

SEE PARALLEL ACCOUNTS AT MARK 14:26, 32–42 AND LUKE 22:39–46

# CHAPTER 11

## Jesus' Arrest, Trial, and Crucifixion

*Jesus was arrested on Thursday night. In a series of trials, He appeared before members of the Jewish high court, which sent Him to the local Roman governor for sentencing. Condemned to death by Pilate, He was crucified on Friday morning, buried in a borrowed tomb before nightfall, and resurrected early on Sunday morning.*

## 214. JESUS IS ARRESTED

And Judas, who betrayed Him, also knew the place, for Jesus often met there with His disciples. Then Judas, having received a band of men and officers from the chief priests and Pharisees, came there with lanterns and torches and weapons.

Therefore Jesus, knowing all things that would come on Him, went forth and said to them, "Whom do you seek?"

They answered Him, "Jesus of Nazareth."

### A SEVERED EAR HEALED

This account of the arrest of Jesus also appears in Matthew (26:47–56), Mark (14:43–50), and Luke (22:47–53). Thus, all four Gospels report that the ear of Malchus was severed by a disciple, but only Luke reveals that Jesus "touched his ear and healed him" (Luke 22:51).

Jesus said to them, "I am He." And Judas, who betrayed Him, also stood with them. Then as soon as He had said to them, "I am He," they went backward and fell to the ground.

Then He asked them again, "Whom do you seek?"

And they said, "Jesus of Nazareth."

Jesus answered, "I have told you that I am He. Therefore, if you seek Me, let these go their way," that the saying that He spoke might be fulfilled, "I have lost none of those whom You gave Me."

Then Simon Peter, having a sword, drew it and struck the high priest's servant, and cut off his right ear. The servant's name was Malchus. Then Jesus said to Peter, "Put up your sword into the sheath. Shall I not drink the cup that My Father has given Me?"

Then the cohort and the captain and officers of the Jews took Jesus and bound Him. *John 18:2–12*

## 215. QUESTIONING BY ANNAS, THE FORMER HIGH PRIEST

Then the cohort and the captain and officers of the Jews took Jesus and bound Him and led Him away first to Annas, for he was father-in-law to Caiaphas, who was the high priest that same year. Now Caiaphas was he who gave counsel to the Jews that it was expedient that one man should die for the people. *John 18:12–14*

The high priest then asked Jesus about His disciples and about His doctrine. Jesus answered him, "I spoke openly to the world. I always taught in the synagogue and in the temple, where the Jews always meet, and I have said nothing in secret.

Jesus restrains Peter from further violence against the high priest's servant, Malchus.

Why do you ask Me? Ask those who heard Me what I have said to them. Behold, they know what I said."

And when He had said this, one of the officers who stood by struck Jesus with the palm of his hand, saying, "Do You answer the high priest like that?"

Jesus answered him, "If I have spoken evil, bear witness of the evil, but if well, why did you strike Me?" *John 18:19–23*

## 216. APPEARANCE BEFORE CAIAPHAS, THE CURRENT HIGH PRIEST

And those who had taken hold of Jesus led Him away to Caiaphas the high priest, where the scribes and the elders were assembled. But Peter followed Him afar off to the high priest's palace and went in and sat with the servants to see the end.

Now the chief priests, and elders, and all the council sought false witness against Jesus to put Him to death, but found none. Yes, though many false witnesses came, yet they found none. At the last came two false witnesses and said, "This fellow said, 'I am able to destroy the temple of God and to build it in three days.'"

And the high priest arose and said to Him, "Do You answer nothing? What is it that these men testify against You?" But Jesus remained silent. And the high priest answered and said to Him, "I adjure You by the living God, that You tell us whether You are the Christ, the Son of God."

Jesus said to him, "You have said it. Nevertheless, I say to you, hereafter you shall see the Son of Man sitting on the right hand of Power and coming in the clouds of heaven."

Then the high priest tore his clothes, saying, "He has spoken blasphemy. What further need do we have of witnesses? Behold, now you have heard His blasphemy. What do you think?"

They answered and said, "He is guilty of death."

Then they spit in His face and beat Him, and others struck Him with the palms of their hands, saying, "Prophesy to us, Christ. Who is he who struck You?" *Matthew 26:57–68*

## 217. PETER'S DENIAL OF JESUS

Then they took Him [Jesus], and led Him, and brought Him into the high priest's house. And Peter followed afar off. And when they had kindled a fire in the midst of the hall and had sat down together, Peter sat down among them. But a certain maid saw him as he sat by the fire, and earnestly looked at him, and said, "This man was also with Him."

And he denied Him, saying, "Woman, I do not know Him."

And after a little while another saw him and said, "You also are of them."

Pressured by accusers, Peter declares that he is not a disciple of Jesus.

And Peter said, "Man, I am not."

And about the space of one hour after, another confidently affirmed, saying, "Truly this fellow also was with Him, for he is a Galilean."

And Peter said, "Man, I do not know what you are saying."

And immediately, while he still spoke, the rooster crowed. And the Lord turned and looked at Peter. And Peter remembered the word of the Lord, how He had said to him, "Before the rooster crows, you shall deny Me three times." And Peter went out and wept bitterly. *Luke 22:54–62*

SEE PARALLEL ACCOUNTS AT MATTHEW 26:58, 69–75;
MARK 14:54, 66–72; AND JOHN 18:15–18, 25–27

221

## 218. THE SANHEDRIN CONDEMNS JESUS

And as soon as it was day, the elders of the people and the chief priests and the scribes came together and led Him into their council, saying, "Are You the Christ? Tell us."

And He said to them, "If I tell you, you will not believe. And if I also ask you, you will not answer Me or let Me go. Hereafter the Son of Man shall sit on the right hand of the power of God."

Then they all said, "Are You then the Son of God?"

And He said to them, "You say that I am."

And they said, "What further witness do we need? For we ourselves have heard from His own mouth." *Luke 22:66–71*

SEE PARALLEL ACCOUNTS AT MATTHEW 27:1–2 AND MARK 15:1

### JESUS BEFORE THE JEWISH COURT

The "council" before which Jesus appeared (see section 218) was the Sanhedrin, the Jewish high court. This judicial body was composed of scribes, elders, and priests, with the high priest as presiding officer. Their charge against Jesus was committing blasphemy by claiming to be God, a capital offense under Jewish law.

This group did not have the authority to carry out the death penalty, so they sent their prisoner to Pilate, the Roman governor, for sentencing. They were determined to have Jesus put to death.

## 219. JUDAS TAKES HIS OWN LIFE

Then Judas, who had betrayed Him [Jesus], when he saw that He was condemned, felt sorrowful and brought back the thirty pieces of silver to the chief priests and elders, saying, "I have sinned in that I have betrayed innocent blood."

And they said, "What is that to us? You see to that."

And he cast down the pieces of silver in the temple and departed, and went and hanged himself.

And the chief priests took the silver pieces and said, "It is not lawful for us to put them into the treasury, because it is the price of blood." And they took counsel and bought with them the potter's field, to bury strangers in. Therefore that field has been called the Field of Blood to this day.

Then what was spoken by Jeremiah the prophet was fulfilled: "And they took the thirty pieces of silver, the price of Him who was valued, whom those of the children of Israel valued, and gave them for the potter's field, as the Lord appointed me." *Matthew 27:3–10*

Jewish religious leaders listen in as Jesus is questioned by Pilate.

## 220. JESUS APPEARS BEFORE PILATE

Then they [members of the Sanhedrin] led Jesus from Caiaphas to the hall of judgment, and it was early. And they themselves did not go into the judgment hall, lest they should be defiled, but that they might eat the Passover. Then Pilate went out to them and said, "What accusation do you bring against this Man?"

They answered and said to him, "If He were not a criminal, we would not have delivered Him up to you."

Then Pilate said to them, "You take Him and judge Him according to your law."

Therefore the Jews said to him, "It is not lawful for us to put any man to death," that the saying of Jesus might be fulfilled that He spoke, signifying what death He should die.

Then Pilate entered into the judgment hall again and called Jesus and said to Him, "Are You the King of the Jews?"

Jesus answered him, "Do you say this thing of yourself, or did others tell it to you of Me?"

Pilate answered, "Am I a Jew? Your own nation and the chief priests have delivered You to me. What have You done?"

### "My Kingdom Is Not from Here"

Jesus answered, "My kingdom is not of this world. If My kingdom were of this world, then My servants would fight, that I should not be delivered to the Jews. But now My kingdom is not from here."

Therefore Pilate said to Him, "Are You a king then?"

Jesus answered, "You say that I am a king. For this purpose I was born, and for this purpose I came into the world, that I should bear witness to the truth. Everyone who is of the truth hears My voice."

Pilate said to Him, "What is truth?" And when he had said this, he went out again to the Jews and said to them, "I find no fault in Him at all." *John 18:28–38*
SEE PARALLEL ACCOUNTS AT MATTHEW 27:2, 11–
14; MARK 15:1–5; AND LUKE 23:1–5

## 221. JESUS SENT TO HEROD ANTIPAS

When Pilate heard of Galilee, he asked whether the man [Jesus] was a Galilean. And as soon as he knew that He belonged to Herod's jurisdiction, he sent Him to Herod, who himself was also in Jerusalem at that time.

And when Herod saw Jesus, he was exceedingly glad, for he had desired to see Him for a long season because he had heard many things about Him, and he hoped to have seen some miracle done by Him.

Then he questioned Him with many words, but He answered him nothing. And the chief priests and scribes stood and vehemently accused Him. And Herod, with his men of war, despised Him and mocked Him, and arrayed Him in a gorgeous robe, and sent Him again to Pilate.

And the same day Pilate and Herod became friends with each other, for before they were at enmity with each other. *Luke 23:6–12*

## 222. FREEDOM FOR BARABBAS— DEATH FOR JESUS

Now at that feast [the Passover] the governor was accustomed to releasing to the people a prisoner whom they wanted. And then they had a notable prisoner called Barabbas. Therefore when they had gathered together, Pilate said to them, "Whom do you want me to release to you? Barabbas or Jesus, who is called Christ?" For he knew that they had delivered Him because of envy.

When he was sitting down on the judgment seat, his wife sent to him, saying, "Have nothing to do with that just Man, for I have suffered many things in a dream this day because of Him."

But the chief priests and elders persuaded the multitude that they should ask for Barabbas and destroy Jesus. The governor answered and said to them, "Which of the two do you want me to release to you?"

They said, "Barabbas."

Pilate said to them, "What then shall I do with Jesus, who is called Christ?"

They all said to him, "Let Him be crucified."

And the governor said, "Why, what evil has He done?"

But they cried out the more, saying, "Let Him be crucified!" *Matthew 27:15–23*
SEE PARALLEL ACCOUNTS AT MARK 15:6–14;
LUKE 23:13–25; AND JOHN 18:39–40

## 223. JESUS MOCKED AND BEATEN

Therefore Pilate then took Jesus and scourged Him. And the soldiers wove a crown of thorns and put it on His head, and they put a purple robe on Him and said, "Hail, King of the Jews!" And they struck Him with their hands.

Therefore Pilate went out again and said to them, "Behold, I bring Him out to you, that you may know that I find no fault in Him."

Then Jesus came out, wearing the crown of thorns and the purple robe. And Pilate said to them, "Behold the Man!"

Therefore when the chief priests and officers saw Him, they cried out, saying, "Crucify Him, crucify Him!"

Pilate said to them, "You take Him and crucify Him, for I find no fault in Him."

The Jews answered him, "We have a law, and by our law He ought to die because He made Himself the Son of God."

Therefore when Pilate heard that saying, he was even more afraid, and went into the judgment hall again, and said to Jesus, "Where are You from?" But Jesus

Jesus wears a crown of thorns while Roman soldiers mockingly bow to Him.

gave him no answer. Then Pilate said to Him, "Will You not speak to me? Do You not know that I have power to crucify You and have power to release You?"

Jesus answered, "You would have no power at all against Me unless it were given you from above. Therefore he who delivered Me to you has the greater sin." *John 19:1–11*

SEE PARALLEL ACCOUNTS AT MATTHEW 27:26–31 AND MARK 15:16–20

## 224. PILATE CONDEMNS JESUS TO BE CRUCIFIED

And from then on Pilate sought to release Him [Jesus], but the Jews cried out, saying, "If you let this Man go, you are not Caesar's friend. Whoever makes himself a king speaks against Caesar."

Therefore when Pilate heard that saying, he brought Jesus out and sat down in the judgment seat in a place that is called the Pavement, but in the Hebrew, Gabbatha. And it was the preparation of the Passover and about the sixth hour. And he said to the Jews, "Behold your King!"

But they cried out, "Away with Him, away with Him, crucify Him!"

Pilate said to them, "Shall I crucify your King?"

The chief priests answered, "We have no king but Caesar."

Therefore he then delivered Him to them to be crucified. And they took Jesus and led Him away. *John 19:12–16*

Pilate tries to dodge responsibility for his execution order against Jesus.

## 225. PILATE WASHES HIS HANDS OF JESUS' BLOOD

When Pilate saw that he could prevail nothing, but rather that a tumult was made, he took water and washed his hands before the multitude, saying, "I am innocent of the blood of this just Person. You see to it."

Then all the people answered and said, "His blood be on us and on our children." *Matthew 27:24–25*

## 226. JESUS WARNS ABOUT THE PERILOUS DAYS TO COME

And as they led Him [Jesus] away, they laid hold on one Simon, a Cyrenian, coming out of the country, and they laid the cross on him, that he might bear it after Jesus. And a great company of people followed Him, and women who also mourned and lamented Him.

But Jesus, turning to them, said, "Daughters of Jerusalem, do not weep for Me, but weep for yourselves and for your children. For behold, the days are coming in which they shall say, 'Blessed are the barren, and the wombs that never bore, and the breasts that never nursed.'

"Then they shall begin to say to the mountains, 'Fall on us,' and to the hills, 'Cover us.' For if they do these things in a green tree, what shall be done in the dry?" *Luke 23:26–31*

## 227. THE INSCRIPTION ON JESUS' CROSS

And He [Jesus], bearing His cross, went out to a place called the place of a skull, which is called in the Hebrew, Golgotha, where they crucified Him and two others with Him, one on either side, and Jesus in the middle.

And Pilate wrote a title and put it on the cross. And the writing was JESUS OF NAZARETH THE KING OF THE JEWS. Many of the Jews then read this title, for the place where Jesus was crucified was near to the city. And it was written in Hebrew and Greek and Latin.

### A PLACE CALLED CALVARY

John's Gospel calls the crucifixion site by its Aramaic name, Golgotha (see section 227). But the Gospel of Luke refers to it as Calvary, its Latin name (Luke 23:33). This "place of a skull" is a rocky cliff face just outside the walls of the Old City of Jerusalem. Its deep crevices bear a resemblance to a human skull. The site was first identified by British general Charles Gordon in 1863. It is sometimes referred to as "Gordon's Calvary."

Then the chief priests of the Jews said to Pilate, "Do not write, 'The King of the Jews,' but that 'He said, "I am King of the Jews."'"

Pilate answered, "What I have written, I have written." *John 19:17–22*

SEE PARALLEL ACCOUNTS AT MATTHEW 27:36–37, MARK 15:25–26, AND LUKE 23:38

Pilate and religious leaders discuss the placard posted on Jesus' cross.

## 228. SOLDIERS CAST LOTS FOR JESUS' CLOTHES

Then the soldiers, when they had crucified Jesus, took His garments and made four parts, for every soldier a part, and also His coat. Now the coat was without seam, woven from the top throughout.

Therefore they said among themselves, "Let us not tear it but cast lots for it to see whose it shall be," that the scripture might be fulfilled that says, "They parted My garments among them, and they cast lots for My clothing." Therefore the soldiers did these things. *John 19:23–24*

229

## 229. JESUS TAUNTED FOR REFUSING TO SAVE HIMSELF

And those who passed by reviled Him [Jesus], shaking their heads and saying, "You who destroy the temple and build it in three days, save Yourself. If You are the Son of God, come down from the cross."

Likewise the chief priests also, mocking Him with the scribes and elders, said, "He saved others; He cannot save Himself. If He is the King of Israel, let Him come down now from the cross, and we will believe Him. He trusted in God; let Him deliver Him now if He will have Him. For He said, 'I am the Son of God.'"
*Matthew 27:39–43*

SEE PARALLEL ACCOUNTS AT MARK 15:29–32 AND LUKE 23:35–37

## 230. A DYING CRIMINAL TURNS TO JESUS

And one of the criminals who was hanged [along with Jesus] railed on Him, saying, "If You are Christ, save Yourself and us."

But the other, answering, rebuked him, saying, "Do you not fear God, seeing you are in the same condemnation? And we indeed justly, for we receive the due reward of our deeds. But this man has done nothing wrong." And he said to Jesus, "Lord, remember me when You come into Your kingdom."

And Jesus said to him, "Truly I say to you, today you shall be with Me in paradise." *Luke 23:39–43*

SEE PARALLEL ACCOUNTS AT MATTHEW 27:38, 44 AND MARK 15:27–28

### JESUS' FINAL WORDS

This assurance of Jesus to a condemned criminal (see section 230) was one of several utterances that He made from the cross. The others were:

- "Father, forgive them; for they do not know what they do" (Luke 23:34).
- To His mother: "Woman, behold your son." To His disciple John: "Behold your mother!" (John 19:26–27).
- "I thirst" (John 19:28).
- "My God, my God, why have You forsaken Me?" (Matthew 27:46; Mark 15:34).
- "It is finished" (John 19:30).
- "Father, into Your hands I commend My spirit" (Luke 23:46).

From the cross,
Jesus commends His
mother to the care of
His disciple John.

## 231. JESUS ASKS JOHN TO CARE FOR HIS MOTHER

Now by the cross of Jesus stood His mother, and His mother's sister, Mary the wife of Clopas, and Mary Magdalene. Therefore when Jesus saw His mother and the disciple whom He loved standing by, He said to His mother, "Woman, behold, your son!"

Then He said to the disciple, "Behold, your mother!" And from that hour that disciple took her to his own home. *John 19:25–27*

## 232. A CRY OF SORROW FROM THE CROSS

Now from the sixth hour to the ninth hour there was darkness over all the land. And about the ninth hour Jesus cried with a loud voice, saying, "Eli, Eli, lama sabachthani?"—that is to say, "My God, My God, why have You forsaken Me?"

Some of those who stood there, when they heard that, said, "This man is calling for Elijah." And immediately one of them ran and took a sponge, and filled it with vinegar, and put it on a reed, and gave Him a drink.

The rest said, "Leave Him alone. Let us see whether Elijah will come to save Him."

Jesus, when He had cried again with a loud voice, gave up His spirit. *Matthew 27:45–50*

## 233. DRAMATIC EVENTS AT JESUS' DEATH

And, behold, the veil of the temple was torn in two from the top to the bottom. And the earth quaked, and the rocks split, and the graves were opened. And many bodies of the saints who slept arose, and came out of the graves after His resurrection, and went into the holy city and appeared to many.

Now when the centurion and those who were with him, watching Jesus, saw the earthquake and those things that had been done, they feared greatly, saying, "Truly this was the Son of God." *Matthew 27:51–54*

### TWO PROPHECIES FULFILLED

According to John's account of the sword thrust into Jesus' side (see section 234), this event fulfilled two Old Testament prophecies:

- "He keeps all his bones. Not one of them is broken" (Psalm 34:20).
- "They shall look at Me whom they have pierced" (Zechariah 12:10).

Therefore, because it was the day of preparation, that the bodies should not remain on the cross on the Sabbath day (for that Sabbath day was a high day), the Jews asked Pilate that their legs might be broken, and that they might be taken away.

Then the soldiers came and broke the legs of the first and of the other who was crucified with Him. But when they came to Jesus and saw that He was dead already, they did not break His legs. But one of the soldiers with a spear pierced His side, and immediately blood and water came out.

A Roman centurion marvels at the mysterious events surrounding Jesus' death.

And he who saw it has borne witness, and his witness is true, and he knows that what he says is true, that you might believe. For these things were done that the scripture should be fulfilled: "No bone of His shall be broken." And again another scripture says, "They shall look on Him whom they pierced." *John 19:31–37*

## 235. JOSEPH AND NICODEMUS BURY JESUS' BODY

And after this, Joseph of Arimathea, being a disciple of Jesus, but secretly, for fear of the Jews, asked Pilate that he might take away the body of Jesus, and Pilate gave him permission. Therefore he came and took the body of Jesus.

And Nicodemus, who at first came to Jesus by night, also came and brought a mixture of myrrh and aloes, weighing about a hundred pounds. Then they took the body of Jesus and wound it in linen cloths with the spices to bury, as is the manner of the Jews.

Now in the place where He was crucified there was a garden, and in the garden a new sepulchre, in which no man was yet laid. Therefore they laid Jesus there because of the Jews' preparation day, for the sepulchre was nearby. *John 19:38–42*

### BURIAL IN JOSEPH'S TOMB

Accounts of Jesus' burial also appear in Matthew (27:57–60), Mark (15:42–46), and Luke (23:50–53). These Gospels make it clear that His burial was in a new tomb that had never been used. But only Matthew reports that this tomb belonged to Joseph of Arimathea (Matthew 27:59–60).

## 236. WOMEN NOTE THE BURIAL PLACE

And also the women who came with Him from Galilee followed after and saw the sepulchre and how His body was laid. And they returned and prepared spices and ointments. And they rested on the Sabbath day according to the commandment. *Luke 23:55–56*

SEE PARALLEL ACCOUNTS AT MATTHEW 27:61 AND MARK 15:47

## 237. SECURITY PRECAUTIONS AT THE TOMB

Now the next day, which followed the day of the preparation, the chief priests and Pharisees came together to Pilate, saying, "Sir, we remember, while He was yet alive, that deceiver said, 'After three days I will rise again.' Therefore command that the sepulchre be made secure until the third day, lest His disciples come by night and steal Him away, and say to the people, 'He has risen from the dead.' So the last error shall be worse than the first."

Pilate said to them, "You have a guard. Go your way. Make it as secure as you can." So they went and made the sepulchre secure, sealing the stone, and setting a guard. *Matthew 27:62–66*

Jesus' body is carried away for burial in the tomb of Joseph of Arimathea.

# CHAPTER 12

## Jesus' Resurrection and Ascension

*After His resurrection, Jesus appeared to His disciples and other followers over a period of forty days (Acts 1:3). These appearances assured them that He was alive and would continue to strengthen them through His spiritual presence. He ascended to God the Father with the promise that He would return at some future day. Meanwhile, they should continue the work of spiritual redemption that God sent Him into the world to do.*

At the end of the Sabbath, as it began to dawn toward the first day of the week, Mary Magdalene and the other Mary came to see the sepulchre. And behold, there was a great earthquake, for the angel of the Lord descended from heaven, and came and rolled back the stone from the door, and sat on it. His face was like lightning, and his clothing white as snow. And the guards shook for fear of him and became as dead men.

And the angel answered and said to the women, "Do not fear, for I know that you seek Jesus, who was crucified. He is not here, for He has risen, as He said. Come, see the place where the Lord lay. And go quickly and tell His disciples that He has risen from the dead. And behold, He is going before you to Galilee. You shall see Him there. Behold, I have told you."

And they departed quickly from the sepulchre with fear and great joy, and ran to bring His disciples word. *Matthew 28:1–8*

See parallel accounts at Mark 16:1–8; Luke 24:1–8; and John 20:1–2

An angel informs women at the tomb that Jesus has been resurrected.

## THE WOMEN AT JESUS' TOMB

All four Gospels report that several women followers of Jesus were the first to discover that He had risen from the dead. They came to the burial site to anoint His body with spices to give Him a decent burial.

A careful comparison of these Gospel accounts—Matthew 28:1; Mark 16:1; Luke 24:10; and John 20:1—reveals who these women were: Mary Magdalene, Salome, Mary the mother of James, and Joanna. Only John's Gospel tells us that Mary Magdalene came alone to the tomb, where the risen Jesus appeared and talked with her (see section 240).

The first day of the week Mary Magdalene came to the sepulchre early, when it was still dark, and saw the stone taken away from the sepulchre. Then she ran and came to Simon Peter and to the other disciple, whom Jesus loved, and said to them, "They have taken away the Lord out of the sepulchre, and we do not know where they have laid Him."

Therefore Peter and that other disciple went out and went to the sepulchre.

So they both ran together, and the other disciple outran Peter and came to the sepulchre first. And he, stooping down and looking in, saw the linen cloths lying there, yet he did not go in.

Then Simon Peter came, following him, and went into the sepulchre and saw the linen cloths lying there, and the cloth that was around His head not lying with the linen clothes but wrapped together in a place by itself.

Then that other disciple, who came first to the sepulchre, also went in, and he saw and believed. For as yet they did not know the scripture, that He must rise again from the dead. Then the disciples went away again to their own homes.
*John 20:1–10*

SEE PARALLEL ACCOUNT
AT LUKE 24:9–12

Peter and John hurry to check out
the report of the empty tomb.

## 240. MARY MAGDALENE ENCOUNTERS JESUS

But Mary stood outside the sepulchre weeping, and as she wept she stooped down and looked into the sepulchre. And she saw two angels in white sitting, the one at the head and the other at the feet, where the body of Jesus had lain. And they said to her, "Woman, why are you weeping?"

She said to them, "Because they have taken away my Lord, and I do not know where they have laid Him."

And when she had said this, she turned herself back and saw Jesus standing there, and did not know that it was Jesus. Jesus said to her, "Woman, why are you weeping? Whom do you seek?"

Supposing Him to be the gardener, she said to Him, "Sir, if You have carried Him from here, tell me where You have laid Him, and I will take Him away."

Jesus said to her, "Mary."

She turned herself and said to Him, "Rabboni" (which is to say, Master).

Jesus said to her, "Do not touch Me, for I have not yet ascended to My Father, but go to My brothers and say to them, 'I am ascending to My Father and your Father, and to My God and your God.'" *John 20:11–17*

SEE PARALLEL ACCOUNT AT MARK 16:9–11

## 241. A FALSE CLAIM ABOUT JESUS' BODY

And when they [members of the Sanhedrin] had assembled with the elders and had taken counsel, they gave a large amount of money to the soldiers, saying, "Say, 'His disciples came by night and stole Him away while we slept.' And if this comes to the governor's ears, we will persuade him and secure you."

So they took the money and did as they were instructed. And this saying is commonly reported among the Jews until this day. *Matthew 28:12–15*

## 242. A CONVERSATION ON THE ROAD TO EMMAUS

And, behold, two of them [followers of Jesus] went that same day [the day of Jesus' resurrection] to a village called Emmaus, which was about sixty furlongs from Jerusalem. And they talked together of all these things that had happened. And it came to pass, that while they spoke and reasoned together, Jesus Himself drew near and went with them. But their eyes were covered, that they would not know Him.

And He said to them, "What manner of communications are these that you have with one another as you walk and are sad?"

And the one of them, whose name was Cleopas, answered and said to Him, "Are You only a stranger in Jerusalem, and have not known the things that have come to pass there in these days?"

And He said to them, "What things?"

And they said to Him, "Concerning Jesus of Nazareth, who was a prophet mighty in deed and word before God and all the people, and how the chief priests and our rulers delivered Him to be condemned to death, and have crucified Him. But we trusted that it was He who would have redeemed Israel. And besides all this, today is the third day since these things were done.

"Yes, and some women also of our company, who were at the sepulchre early, made us astonished. And when they did not find His body, they came saying that they had also seen a vision of angels who said that He was alive. And some of those who were with us went to the sepulchre and found it even so as the women had said, but they did not see Him."

## "O Fools, and Slow. . .to Believe"

Then He said to them, "O fools, and slow of heart to believe all that the prophets have spoken. Ought not Christ to have suffered these things and to enter into His glory?" And beginning at Moses and all the prophets, He expounded to them the things concerning Himself in all the scriptures.

And they drew near to the village where they went, and He made as though He would have gone farther. But they urged Him, saying, "Stay with us, for it is toward evening, and the day is far spent." And He went in to stay with them.

The resurrected Jesus breaks bread with two followers at Emmaus.

And it came to pass, as He sat at the table with them, He took bread and blessed and broke it, and gave to them. And their eyes were opened and they knew Him. And He vanished out of their sight.

## "They Rose Up. . .and Returned to Jerusalem"

And they said to one another, "Did not our hearts burn within us while He talked with us on the road and while He opened the scriptures to us? And they rose up the same hour and returned to Jerusalem and found the eleven [disciples of Jesus] and those who were with them gathered together, saying, "The Lord has risen indeed and has appeared to Simon."

And they told about the things that were done on the road, and how He was known to them in the breaking of bread. *Luke 24:13–35*

SEE PARALLEL ACCOUNT AT MARK 16:12–13

## 243. JESUS APPEARS TO HIS DISCIPLES IN JERUSALEM

And as they [Jesus' disciples] were saying this, Jesus Himself stood in their midst and said to them, "Peace be to you." But they were terrified and frightened and supposed that they had seen a spirit. And He said to them, "Why are you troubled? And why do thoughts arise in your hearts? Behold My hands and My feet, that it is I Myself. Touch Me and see, for a spirit does not have flesh and bones as you see I have."

And when He had said this, He showed them His hands and His feet. And while they still did not believe for joy and wondered, He said to them, "Have you any food here?" And they gave Him a piece of a broiled fish and of a honeycomb. And He took it and ate before them.

And He said to them, "These are the words that I spoke to you while I was still with you, that all things must be fulfilled that were written in the law of Moses and in the Prophets and in the Psalms concerning Me."

Then He opened their understanding, that they might understand the scriptures, and said to them, "So it is written, and thus it was necessary for Christ to suffer and to rise from the dead the third day." *Luke 24:36–46*

SEE PARALLEL ACCOUNTS AT MARK 16:14 AND JOHN 20:19–23

## 244. DOUBTING THOMAS BECOMES A BELIEVER

Then at evening the same day [of Jesus' resurrection], being the first day of the week, when the doors were shut where the disciples were assembled, for fear of the Jews, Jesus came and stood in the midst and said to them, "Peace be to you."

And when He had said this, He showed them His hands and His side. Then the disciples were glad when they saw the Lord. *John 20:19–20*

But Thomas, called Didymus, one of the twelve, was not with them when Jesus came. Therefore the other disciples said to him, "We have seen the Lord."

But he said to them, "Unless I see in His hands the print of the nails, and put my finger into the print of the nails, and thrust my hand into His side, I will not believe."

And after eight days His disciples were again inside, and Thomas with them. Then Jesus came, the doors being shut, and stood in the midst, and said, "Peace be to you." Then He said to Thomas, "Reach your finger here, and behold My hands. And reach your hand here and thrust it into My side. And do not be faithless, but believing."

And Thomas answered and said to Him, "My Lord and my God."

Jesus said to him, "Thomas, because you have seen Me, you have believed. Blessed are those who have not seen and yet have believed." *John 20:24–29*

After seeing the resurrected Jesus with his own eyes, Thomas declared, "My Lord and my God."

# 245. JESUS APPEARS TO SEVEN DISCIPLES AT THE SEA OF GALILEE

After these things Jesus again showed Himself to the disciples at the Sea of Tiberias, and He showed Himself in this way. There were together Simon Peter, and Thomas called Didymus, and Nathanael of Cana in Galilee, and the sons of Zebedee, and two others of His disciples.

Simon Peter said to them, "I am going fishing."

They said to him, "We will also go with you." They went out and immediately entered into a ship, and that night they caught nothing.

But when the morning had come, Jesus stood on the shore, but the disciples did not know that it was Jesus. Then Jesus said to them, "Children, do you have any food?"

They answered Him, "No."

And He said to them, "Cast the net on the right side of the ship, and you shall find some." Therefore they cast, and now they were not able to draw it for the multitude of fish.

Therefore that disciple whom Jesus loved said to Peter, "It is the Lord." Now when Simon Peter heard that it was the Lord, he put on his fisher's coat (for he was naked) and cast himself into the sea.

And the other disciples came in a little ship (for they were not far from land, but about two hundred cubits away), dragging the net with fish. Then as soon as they had come to land, they saw a fire of coals there and fish laid on it and bread.

Jesus said to them, "Bring some of the fish that you have now caught." Simon Peter went up and dragged to land the net full of great fish, a hundred and fifty-three. And although there were so many, still the net was not broken.

Jesus said to them, "Come and dine."

And none of the disciples dared ask Him, "Who are You?" knowing that it was the Lord. Then Jesus came and took bread and gave it to them, and likewise fish. This is now the third time that Jesus showed Himself to His disciples after He was raised from the dead. *John 21:1–14*

## FISH FOR A SHARED MEAL

This account of a large catch of fish (see section 245) is similar to the miraculous catch that Jesus produced at the beginning of His ministry. The first occurred when He called two sets of fishermen brothers to become His disciples (see section 34).

But most interpreters don't consider this second catch a miracle. Jesus simply told Peter to cast his net in a spot where fish had been spotted. John may have included this account in His Gospel to disprove the rumor that Jesus was nothing more than a vision or hallucination seen by His followers.

Only a man who existed in the flesh could detect fish in the water, then build a fire to cook them on, and enjoy a meal of fresh fish with His disciples.

After His resurrection, Jesus enjoyed a meal of fresh fish with several disciples in Galilee.

## 246. PETER FORGIVEN AND RESTORED

So when they [Jesus' disciples] had dined, Jesus said to Simon Peter, "Simon, son of John, do you love Me more than these?"

He said to Him, "Yes, Lord; You know that I love You."

He said to him, "Feed My lambs."

He said to him again the second time, "Simon, son of John, do you love Me?"

He said to Him, "Yes, Lord; You know that I love You."

He said to him, "Feed My sheep."

He said to him the third time, "Simon, son of John, do you love Me?" Peter was grieved because He said to him the third time, "Do you love Me?"

And he said to Him, "Lord, You know all things; You know that I love You."

Jesus said to him, "Feed My sheep. Truly, truly, I say to you, when you were young, you dressed yourself and walked where you wanted. But when you are old, you shall stretch out your hands and another shall dress you and carry you where you do not want to go."

This He spoke, signifying by what death he should glorify God. And when He had spoken this, He said to him, "Follow Me." *John 21:15–19*

Jesus directs Peter to continue to serve Him and the "sheep" who are His followers.

## 247. WHAT WILL HAPPEN TO THE APOSTLE JOHN?

Then Peter, turning around, saw the disciple whom Jesus loved following, who also leaned on His breast at supper, and said, "Lord, who is he who betrays You?" Peter, seeing him, said to Jesus, "Lord, and what shall this man do?"

Jesus said to him, "If I want him to remain till I come, what is that to you? You follow Me." Then this saying spread among the brothers that that disciple would not die. Yet Jesus did not say to him that he shall not die, but, "If I want him to remain till I come, what is that to you?"

This is the disciple who testifies of these things, and wrote these things, and we know that his testimony is true. *John 21:20–24*

## 248. JESUS CHARGES THE ELEVEN TO CONTINUE HIS WORK

Then the eleven disciples went away into Galilee, to a mountain that Jesus had appointed for them. And when they saw Him, they worshipped Him, but some doubted.

### INTO ALL THE WORLD

This charge of Jesus to His disciples (see section 248) is known as the Great Commission. All four Gospels as well as the book of Acts contain some version of this familiar passage. The others read:

- "Go into all the world and preach the gospel to every creature" (Mark 16:15).
- "Repentance and remission of sins should be preached in His name among all nations, beginning at Jerusalem. And you are witnesses of these things" (Luke 24:47–48).
- "As My Father has sent Me, even so I send you" (John 20:21).
- "You shall receive power after the Holy Spirit has come upon you, and you shall be witnesses to Me both in Jerusalem and in all Judea and in Samaria and to the farthest part of the earth" (Acts 1:8).

And Jesus came and spoke to them, saying, "All power has been given to Me in heaven and on earth. Therefore go and teach all nations, baptizing them in the name of the Father and of the Son and of the Holy Spirit, teaching them to observe all the things that I have commanded you. And behold, I am with you always, even to the end of the world." Amen. *Matthew 28:16–20*

## 249. JESUS' FINAL BLESSING AND ASCENSION

And He [Jesus] led them [His disciples] out as far as to Bethany, and He lifted up His hands and blessed them. And it came to pass, while He blessed them, He was parted from them and was carried up into heaven.

And they worshipped Him, and returned to Jerusalem with great joy, and were continually in the temple praising and blessing God. Amen. *Luke 24:50–53*

## 250. CONCLUSION: BELIEVE AND RECEIVE

And truly Jesus did many other signs in the presence of His disciples, which are not written in this book. But these are written that you might believe that Jesus is the Christ, the Son of God, and that believing you might have life through His name. *John 20:30–31*

The disciples look
on as Jesus ascends
into heaven.

# MAPS

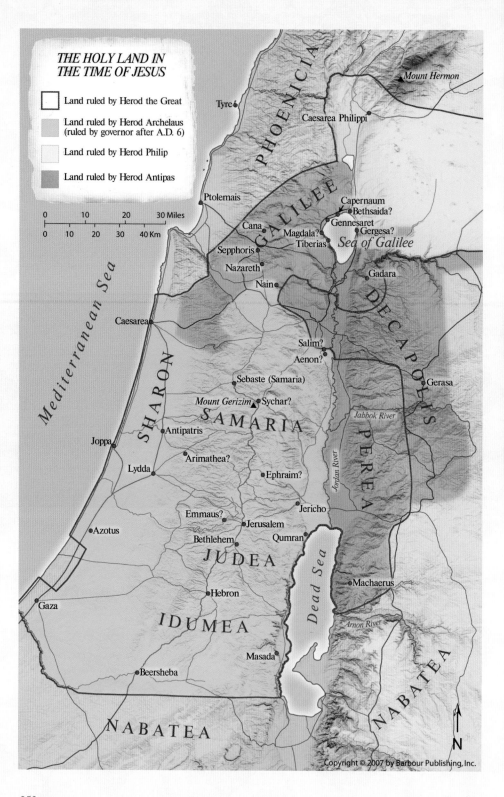

THE HOLY LAND IN
THE TIME OF JESUS

Land ruled by Herod the Great

Land ruled by Herod Archelaus
(ruled by governor after A.D. 6)

Land ruled by Herod Philip

Land ruled by Herod Antipas

0    10    20    30 Miles
0   10   20   30   40 Km

Mount Hermon

Tyre

Caesarea Philippi

PHOENICIA

Ptolemais

GALILEE

Capernaum
Bethsaida?
Gennesaret
Magdala?
Tiberias
Gergesa?
Sea of Galilee

Cana

Sepphoris

Nazareth

Nain

Gadara

DECAPOLIS

Mediterranean Sea

Caesarea

SHARON

Salim?

Aenon?

Gerasa

Sebaste (Samaria)

Mount Gerizim    Sychar?

SAMARIA

PEREA

Jabbok River

Antipatris

Joppa

Arimathea?

Lydda

Ephraim?

Jordan River

Jericho

Emmaus?

Jerusalem

Azotus

Bethlehem

Qumran

JUDEA

Dead Sea

Hebron

Machaerus

Gaza

IDUMEA

Arnon River

Masada

NABATEA

Beersheba

NABATEA

N

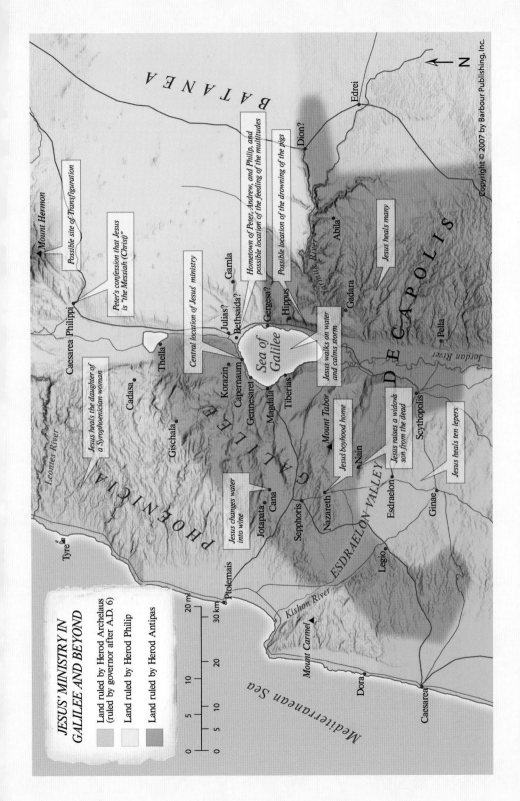

JESUS' MINISTRY IN GALILEE AND BEYOND

Land ruled by Herod Archelaus (ruled by governor after A.D. 6)

Land ruled by Herod Philip

Land ruled by Herod Antipas

Mediterranean Sea

Dora

Caesarea

Mount Carmel

Kishon River

ESDRAELON VALLEY

Legio

Esdraelon

Ginae

Nain

Scythopolis

Jesus heals ten lepers

Jesus raises a widow's son from the dead

Jesus' boyhood home

Mount Tabor

Nazareth

Sepphoris

Jotapata

Cana

Jesus changes water into wine

Ptolemais

Tyre

PHOENICIA

Leontes River

Gischala

Cadasa

Thella

Jesus heals the daughter of a Syrophoenician woman

GALILEE

Gennesaret

Korazin

Capernaum

Magdala

Tiberias

Sea of Galilee

Central location of Jesus' ministry

Bethsaida?

Julias?

Gamla

Peter's confession that Jesus is "the Messiah (Christ)"

Caesarea Philippi

Mount Hermon

Possible site of Transfiguration

BATANEA

Edrei

Dion?

Abila

Gadara

Hippus

Pella

Gergesa?

Jesus walks on water and calms storm

Hometown of Peter, Andrew, and Philip, and possible location of the feeding of the multitudes

Possible location of the drowning of the pigs

Jesus heals many

Yarmuk River

Jordan River

DECAPOLIS

N

Copyright © 2007 by Barbour Publishing, Inc.

253

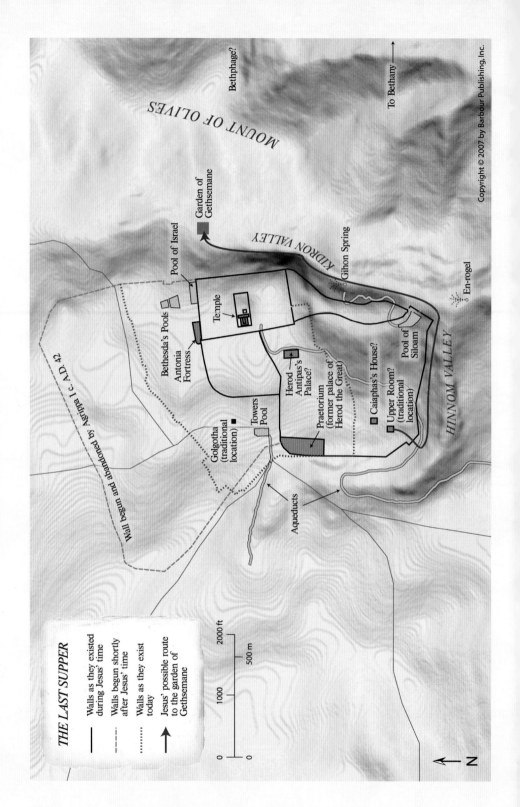

THE LAST SUPPER

Walls as they existed during Jesus' time
Walls begun shortly after Jesus' time
Walls as they exist today
Jesus' possible route to the garden of Gethsemane

N

0   500 m   1000
0   2000 ft

Wall begun and abandoned by Agrippa I c. A.D. 42

Golgotha (traditional location)

Towers Pool

Bethesda's Pools

Antonia Fortress

Temple

Pool of Israel

Garden of Gethsemane

MOUNT OF OLIVES

Bethphage?

To Bethany

Gihon Spring

KIDRON VALLEY

En-rogel

Herod Antipas's Palace?

Praetorium (former palace of Herod the Great)

Caiaphas's House?

Upper Room? (traditional location)

Pool of Siloam

HINNOM VALLEY

Aqueducts

Copyright © 2007 by Barbour Publishing, Inc.

254

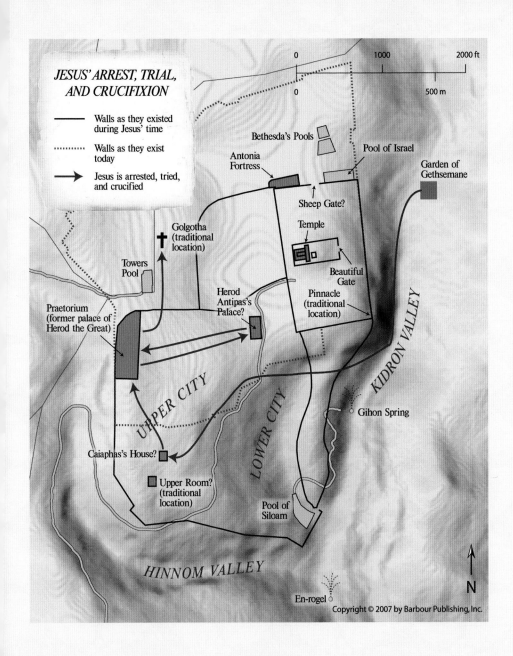

JESUS' ARREST, TRIAL,
AND CRUCIFIXION

——— Walls as they existed
during Jesus' time

·········· Walls as they exist
today

——➤ Jesus is arrested, tried,
and crucified

0          1000          2000 ft
0          500 m

Bethesda's Pools

Antonia
Fortress

Pool of Israel

Garden of
Gethsemane

Sheep Gate?

Temple

Golgotha
(traditional
location)

Towers
Pool

Beautiful
Gate

Praetorium
(former palace of
Herod the Great)

Herod
Antipas's
Palace?

Pinnacle
(traditional
location)

KIDRON VALLEY

UPPER CITY

LOWER CITY

Gihon Spring

Caiaphas's House?

Upper Room?
(traditional
location)

Pool of
Siloam

HINNOM VALLEY

En-rogel

N

Copyright © 2007 by Barbour Publishing, Inc.

# APPENDIX 1:

## MIRACLES OF JESUS
*(in order of appearance in this book)*

Water turned into wine (section 26), p. 47

Royal official's son healed (section 33), p. 58

Miraculous catch of fish (section 34), p. 58

Demon-possessed man healed at Capernaum (section 35), p. 60

Peter's mother-in-law healed (section 36), p. 60

Man healed of leprosy (section 37), p. 61

Lame man healed at Capernaum (section 38), p. 61

Lame man healed at Jerusalem (section 42), p. 64

Man's paralyzed hand healed (section 45), p. 68

Roman centurion's servant healed (section 59), p. 85

Widow's son raised from the dead (section 60), p. 85

Calming of a storm (section 82), p. 98

Demon-possessed man among the tombs healed (section 83), p. 98

Woman with a hemorrhage healed (section 86), p. 100

Jairus's daughter restored to life (section 87), p. 101

Two blind men healed (section 88), p. 102

Deaf man possessed by demons healed (section 89), p. 103

Feeding of the five thousand (section 96), p. 112

Jesus walks on the water (section 97), p. 113

Daughter of a Gentile woman healed (section 103), p. 120

A deaf man healed in Gentile territory (section 104), p. 121

Feeding of four thousand Gentiles (section 105), p. 121

# APPENDIX 2:

## PARABLES OF JESUS

*(in order of appearance in this book)*

House built on a rock (section 58), p. 81

Two debtors (section 67), p. 89

The sower (section 71), p. 91

Candle on a candlestick (section 74), p. 94

Seed growing unseen (section 75), p. 95

Wheat and weeds intermingled (section 76), p. 95

Mustard seed (section 78), p. 96

Leaven in dough (section 79), p. 96

Hidden treasure (section 80), p. 97

A precious pearl (section 80), p. 97

Fishing net (section 81), p. 97

The unforgiving servant (section 117), p. 129

The good Samaritan (section 133), p. 146

A rich but foolish landowner (section 137), p. 149

A fruitless fig tree (section 140), p. 152

The refused invitations (section 147), p. 157

The lost sheep (section 149), p. 159

The lost coin (section 150), p. 160

The lost/prodigal son (section 151), p. 160

The shrewd manager (section 152), p. 162

A rich man and a poor man (section 153), p. 163

The persistent widow (section 161), p. 170

# ART CREDITS:

**125** Renata Sedmakova/Shutterstock

**126** Renata Sedmakova/Shutterstock

**128** Eduardo Estellez/Shutterstock

**130** Luis Santos/Shutterstock

**132–133** John Theodor/Shutterstock

**135** Renata Sedmakova/Shutterstock

**136** Adam Jan Figel/Shutterstock

**139** Renata Sedmakova/Shutterstock

**140** Renata Sedmakova/Shutterstock

**144** Nancy Bauer/Shutterstock

**146** Renata Sedmakova/Shutterstock

**147** Public domain image by French artist James Tissot (1836–1902)

**150** Idan Ben Haim/Shutterstock

**154–155** Ostro/Shutterstock

**156** Kamonrat/Shutterstock

**158** Renata Sedmakova/Shutterstock

**159** mady70/Shutterstock

**161** Adam Jan Figel/Shutterstock

**164** Nicku/Shutterstock

**167** hramikona/Shutterstock

**169** Tiko Aramyan/Shutterstock

**171** ruskpp/Shutterstock

**172** Renata Sedmakova/Shutterstock

**174** Isaac Gil/Shutterstock

**177** Renata Sedmakova/Shutterstock

**178** Public domain

**180–181** kavram/Shutterstock

**183** Onyshchenko/Shutterstock

**185** ruskpp/Shutterstock

**186** Kyna Studio/Shutterstock

**188** tlegend/Shutterstock

**191** Renata Sedmakova/Shutterstock

**192** Renata Sedmakova/Shutterstock

**194** Poleznova/Shutterstock

**196** Nicku/Shutterstock

**198** Public domain image by French artist James Tissot (1836–1902)

**199** Nagel Photography/Shutterstock

**201** Renata Sedmakova/Shutterstock

**203** VP Photo Studio/Shutterstock

**204** jorisvo/Shutterstock

**205** Renata Sedmakova/Shutterstock

**206** Claudio Giovanni Colombo/Shutterstock

**208** Renata Sedmakova/Shutterstock

**212** godongphoto/Shutterstock

**213** Nancy Bauer/Shutterstock

**215** Stig Alenas/Shutterstock

**216–217** Francis OD/Shutterstock

**219** Renata Sedmakova/Shutterstock

**221** Nicku/Shutterstock

**223** Sergieiev/Shutterstock

**226** Freedom Studio/Shutterstock

**227** Renata Sedmakova/Shutterstock

**229** Renata Sedmakova/Shutterstock

**231** Renata Sedmakova/Shutterstock

**233** Renata Sedmakova/Shutterstock

**235** Renata Sedmakova/Shutterstock

**236–237** Jacob_09/Shutterstock

**238** Nancy Bauer/Shutterstock

**239** Public domain image by French artist James Tissot (1836–1902)

**241** Renata Sedmakova/Shutterstock

**243** Adam Jan Figel/Shutterstock

**245** Public domain image by French artist James Tissot (1836–1902)

**246** Renata Sedmakova/Shutterstock

**249** Nancy Bauer/Shutterstock